THE POLITICS OF NATIONAL HEALTH INSURANCE

An Interdisciplinary Research Study

THE POLITICS OF NATIONAL HEALTH INSURANCE: An Interdisciplinary Research Study By Charles J. Austin

Trinity University Press San Antonio

Trinity University Health Services Research Series

Library of Congress Card Catalog Number 75-14975
Printed in the United States of America
Printed by Best Printing Company
Bound by Custom Bookbinders
SBN # 911536-60-4

To Carroll

PREFACE

The debate over establishment of a national health policy constitutes one of the most critical political issues of the 1970's. The previous decade saw the birth of the concept of health care as a right rather than a privilege, a noble goal stated without any practical consideration of the means for carrying it out. The political actors of the 1970's are faced with the difficult task of developing national policies and programs to implement this objective.

This study examines several contemporary approaches to the development of a national health care policy as embodied in five of the major proposals for a system of national health insurance introduced into Congress in 1971 (the research was carried out in late 1971 and early 1972). Since that time, some modifications in the proposals have occurred, but they are still prototypical of the kinds of plans being debated by the Congress in 1975. The research concentrates on the strategies and political behavior inherent in policy debate in an important field.

The size and complexity of the United States health industry is well documented. It employs more than three million people and is estimated to be the third largest industry in the country. Current national health expenditures are in excess of $100 billion per year. The industry is composed of an amalgamation of private and public agencies characterized by a strong tradition of voluntarism as evidenced by the predominance of private, non-profit community hospitals and medical practitioners who operate as private entrepreneurs in the system.

As the health care industry has grown in magnitude and complexity, public attention has been focused on it. Consumers have become increasingly aware of the many problems which beset the system: fragmentation of services, lack of continuity of care, unequal access to health services among various sectors of the population, and, above all, rapidly rising costs.

The pressures resulting from these problems in the health care system have built to the point where some order must be brought from the chaos. It is generally conceded, even by the most extreme of political advocates, that there is an urgent need for a comprehensive national health policy in the United States. The first efforts in this direction are taking the form of proposals for national health insurance. Fifteen such proposals were introduced in the 93rd Congress of the United States.

With the sudden rush toward formulation of national health policy, it is of interest to examine just how carefully the various political advocates are formulating their proposals. To what extent does rational analysis of data support the plans which are being offered?* To what extent are the proposals politically viable? What conflicts are developing between the rational and the political approach to policy development in the field? Questions such as these constitute the subject of the research reported in the pages which follow.

Medical care in this country stands at a critical point. Major new

* Rational policy analysis refers to a system of planning and decision-making characterized by exhaustive cost and benefit analysis of all alternatives. A purely rational system of policy-making would be uninfluenced by special interest group pressure and other forms of political activity and would rely entirely on analytical methods.

legislation is pending before Congress. It would be far too easy to adopt rash legislation that would downgrade the quality of care for both the sick and the healthy. A well-constructed, organized medical care system, based in efficiency and sound economic policy, is essential if we are to meet the needs of a large and complex society. Healthy debate by the various political actors promoting their policies for national health insurance should contribute to this goal, provided that the advocates have done their "homework" and can present reasonable data in support of their positions. The remainder of this book examines just how well that homework is being done.

San Antonio, Texas *Charles J. Austin*
February 1975

CONTENTS

LIST OF TABLES

LIST OF ILLUSTRATIONS

BACKGROUND 1

This study examines the nature of the medical economic data being used to support various proposals for a national health policy, in order to determine the extent to which these proposals are based in sound "rational" analysis as opposed to a design based upon the hidden political agendas of the special interest groups involved. Although much has been written at the theoretical level on the contrasts between rational and political policy analysis, in searching the medical care and policy analysis literature, no other project similar to this one was found.

There is considerable debate in the literature over the question of how "rational" the policy-making process can and should be. The studies of Wildavsky[1] and the works of Braybrooke and Lindblom[2]

[1] Aaron Wildavsky, *The Politics of the Budgetary Process* (Boston: Little, Brown and Company, 1964).

[2] See for example: David Braybrooke and Charles E. Lindblom, *A Strategy of Decision* (New York: The Free Press, 1970), and Charles E. Lindblom, *The Policy Making Process* (Englewood Cliffs, New Jersey: Prentice-Hall Inc., 1968).

(among others) have shown empirically that most of our national policies are developed incrementally through a system of competitive political advocacy.

Lindblom criticizes the purely rational model of decision-making as unworkable.[3] The rational model imposes constraints that cannot be lived with. Policy-makers cannot completely separate goals from means to achieving them, and frequently cannot separate values from facts. Operating with limited time and resources, a decision-maker frequently cannot capture the information required for an exhaustive cost-benefit analysis of all the available alternatives related to a complex policy decision.

Kuhn develops the argument further.[4] Consider a policy or planning decision involving five kinds of benefits and five kinds of costs. Assume that the policy-maker considers only three dimensions connected with each cost and benefit (probability, magnitude, and duration) and ranks each of these dimensions along a five-point scale of measurement (e.g., very probable, probable, uncertain, improbable, very improbable). He then finds himself faced with the problem of analyzing a decision matrix of size 625 by 625 or 390,625 alternatives to be evaluated. The most sophisticated computer equipment and a large staff of qualified analysts could not make such a process practical.

Sharkansky summarizes the barriers to the purely rational decision-making model as follows:

1. The multitude of problems, goals, and policy commitments that are imposed on the administrative unit by those in the environment in which that unit functions,
2. Limits on information on which to make rational assessments,
3. Personal needs, commitments, inhibitions, and inadequacies of administrators,
4. Structural difficulties within administrative units which limit rationality (e.g., conflict between administrative and professional authority),

[3] Charles E. Lindblom, "The Science of Muddling Through," *Public Administration Review* 19 (Spring, 1959): 79–88.

[4] Alfred Kuhn, *The Study of Society: A Unified Approach* (Homewood, Illinois: Irwin-Dorsey Press, 1963), pp. 277–80.

5. Deviant behavior of some administrators.[5]

Lindblom's strategy of successive limited comparisons (referred to as disjointed incrementalism) requires that policy-makers compare and evaluate only increments of policies at the margin.[6] Under this model, administrators consider only a restricted number of alternatives and consequences for any policy decision. They engage in continual readjustment of ends and means, which really cannot be distinguished from one another, anyway. They tend to concentrate on corrective or remedial action in regard to social ills rather than pursuing well-defined future goals.

Under the Lindblom model, policy-making is accomplished through partial mutual adjustment characterized by the absence of cooperation among decision-makers. However, in the advocacy process, every interest has its watchdog (according to Lindblom), and those values which an advocate for one given interest neglects are "mopped-up" by advocates of the neglected values.

Davis, Dempster, and Wildavsky have tested the theory of incrementalism in an empirical study of the federal budgetary process.[7] In examining federal budgetary data for the period 1947 through 1963, they demonstrated that the budget can be described by a series of stochastic, linear models which are stable over periods of time. This year's budget request fits a linear function of last year's appropriation plus a random variable; and for any given agency, the budget prediction becomes more linear over time.

Informed students of policy analysis have not questioned the empirical validity of the Lindblom-Wildavsky models as descriptors of current heuristics in governmental decision-making. However, Lindblom and Wildavsky carry their arguments one step further and contend that the policy-making process *should be* a "non-rational" process, i.e., that their theories are normative as well as descriptive

[5] Ira Sharkansky, *Public Administration* (Markham Publishing Co., 1970), pp. 38–46.

[6] Lindblom, "The Science of Muddling Through," p. 79–88.

[7] Otto A. Davis, M.A.H. Dempster, and Aaron Wildavsky, "A Theory of the Budgetary Process," *The American Political Science Review* 60 (September, 1966): 529–545.

of current practice. On this point there is considerable disagreement among social scientists.

In his "mixed scanning" theory, Etzioni calls for a compromise between the rational and incremental models.[8] Policy-making should be separated into: (1) fundamental decisions—major goals and long-range policies which guide operations and are analyzed rationally at periodic intervals; and (2) short-range, operational decisions which are reached incrementally. Etzioni likens his theory to that of the chess player who plans his strategy several steps ahead, while not attempting to examine all possible strategies which would be clearly impossible.

Etzioni points out that a totally rational approach to decision-making requires more resources than are available to the decision-maker, and the incremental strategy promotes decisions which neglect basic societal problems and innovations. The mixed scanning model tends to reduce the impractical aspects of rationalism by limiting detailed analysis to fundamental decisions only. At the same time, it is far less conservative in its approach since long-range alternatives are explored in detail and reviewed periodically.

Critics of disjointed incrementalism contend that when it is applied over long periods of time, it reinforces the *status quo* and makes meaningful change unlikely. Enid Schoettle in reviewing Lindblom's work argues that the advocacy process does not necessarily bring about optimal decisions.[9] One cannot assume that the advocacy process will always produce the information about program inputs and outputs which are necessary to an informed decision. Furthermore, incrementalism is frequently subject to organizational bias:

> There are, however, frequently situations in which the structure of interests permits only limited values to be represented and constitutes an on going organizational bias against alternate distributions of power. Since specialized bureaucracies consist-

[8] Amitai Etzioni, "Mixed Scanning: A Third Approach to Decision-Making," *Public Administration Review* (December, 1967): 385–92.

[9] Enid C. B. Schoettle. Book review of *The Intelligence of Democracy* and *The Policy-Making Process* by Charles E. Lindblom. *The American Political Science Review* 64 (1970): 1268–72.

> ently initiate policy, and unorganized, apolitical, or poor interests consistently lack well-established access to the policy-making process, such organizational bias frequently prevails and excludes the consideration of certain political values and policy alternatives.[10]

The incremental approach guards against radical departures, but what about those situations in which radical change is needed? In discussing this phase of the problem, Lowi contends that incrementalism becomes manipulative of the public interest.[11] If the character of the choices to be made in the policy making process are not analyzed, then one need not ask any questions about the impact of these choices upon the processes themselves or upon society at large.

Organizations are the instruments through which policies are carried out. Bennis and Slater argue that organizations of the future must be adaptable to rapid change:

> The social structure of organizations of the future will have some unique characteristics. The key word will be "temporary." There will be adaptive, rapidly changing temporary systems . . . of diverse specialists, linked together by coordinating and task-evaluating executive specialists in an organic flux—this is the organization form that will gradually replace bureaucracy as we know it.[12]

However, if public organizations are to become the instruments of rapid social change, then our system of national policy must be based upon analysis and planning sufficient to lead us towards the appropriate organizational forms required by a fast-moving, technological society.

Frederick Mosher also discusses the effects of rational policy analysis on public organizations.[13] He predicts that public agencies will increasingly depend upon the use of analytical techniques in planning and evaluating public programs and that a broadened

[10] *Ibid.*

[11] Theodore Lowi, "Decision Making vs. Policy Making: Toward an Antidote for Technocracy," *Public Administration Review* (May–June, 1970).

[12] Warren G. Bennis and Phillip E. Slater, *The Temporary Society* (New York: Harper and Row, 1968), pp. 73–74.

[13] Frederick C. Mosher, "The Public Service in the Temporary Society," *Public Administration Review* (Jan.–Feb., 1971): 47–62.

and more sophisticated approach to the use of analytical techniques will be developed which will take into account qualitative elements in addition to purely economic factors.

Some limited work has been done on systems of social indicators as an aid to more analytical policy-making in the social sciences. Bauer's examination of the social effects of the space program is probably the most complete work to date on this subject.[14] Included in Bauer's book is Biderman's study of the statement of national goals as embodied in the Report of the President's Commission on National Goals, 1960.[15] Biderman matched major national statistical sources to the statement of goals contained in this report. The results were rather disappointing in that he was unable to match relevant indicators to many of the national goals as stated by the Commission.

My own review of national health indicators suggests that much national health policy is based upon a system of outmoded health statistics and social indicators. I question the readiness of health policy-makers to accept the challenge of using more rational data, relevant to well-identified modern health problems, in the establishment of a national social policy for health.[16]

In response to a directive from President Lyndon B. Johnson in 1966, the Secretary of Health, Education and Welfare appointed a committee to search for ways to improve the nation's ability to chart its social progress and to develop a system of social indicators. The work of this Committee resulted in the document, *Toward a Social Report*, which the Committee produced in 1969.[17] This report, developed by a distinguished panel of social scientists from government, universities, and the private sector, is devoted primarily to a discussion of why social indicators are needed and a description of the deficiencies in our present reporting system. However, the Report does an inadequate job of outlining the characteristics of an

[14] Raymond A. Bauer, ed. *Social Indicators* (Cambridge, Mass.: The M.I.T. Press, 1966).

[15] A. D. Biderman, "Social Indicators and Goals," in *Social Indicators, ibid.*

[16] Charles J. Austin, "Selected Social Indicators in the Health Field," *American Journal of Public Health* 61 (August, 1971): 1507–13.

[17] Wilbur J. Cohen, *Toward a Social Report* (Washington, D.C.: U. S. Department of Health, Education and Welfare, 1969).

improved system of social accounting to improve the policy-making process.

To summarize, the use of social indicators for developing and evaluating health policy is in a very primitive state. This appears to be the result of lack of sophistication in the development of health indicators and also reluctance on the part of political advocates to see such indicators developed and used. Daniel Moynihan is even more pessimistic. He states that social scientists should not be involved in the formulation of social policy, but rather should limit their efforts to attempts to measure the results of such policies.[18]

This study examines the policy-making process in relation to the costs and financing of health care in the United States. A wealth of medical economic literature deals with the costs of health care and the mechanisms for financing the delivery of health services.

Odin Anderson's book, The *Uneasy Equilibrium*, discusses the history of private and public financing of health services in the United States through 1965.[19] Anderson shows how the health services system evolved within the American political, economic, and social environment with particular attention to the impact of scientific advances on the delivery of health services. In his concluding chapter, he discusses the trend toward increased public financing of medical care and alternative approaches to universal health insurance.

Klarman's *The Economics of Health* is a complete treatise on the health care financing system as viewed by an economist.[20] He discusses the factors influencing demand for health services, the factors influencing supply of manpower and facilities, and the results of the demand and supply factors on the organization and regulation of the health industry.

[18] Daniel P. Moynihan, *Maximum Feasible Misunderstanding* (New York: The Free Press, 1970), p. 193.

[19] Odin W. Anderson, *The Uneasy Equilibrium: Private and Public Financing of Health Services in the United States, 1875–1965* (New Haven: College and University Press, 1968).

[20] Herbert E. Klarman, *The Economics of Health* (New York: Columbia University Press, 1965).

Anne Somers in *Health Care in Transition* discusses the problem of increasing expenditures for health care with insurance mechanisms constituting one of the major factors in spiraling costs.[21] Shortcomings and gaps in insurance policies have forced physicians and their patients to use more expensive facilities for treatment (which are covered by the patient's health insurance) when less expensive methods would suffice. Unnecessary hospitalization occurs because health insurance plans usually do not cover out-of-hospital diagnosis and treatment.

Much of the current interest in national health policy deals with *new* proposals for the financing of health care. In the 1971 Michael M. Davis lecture, Isidores Falk calls for the development of a national medical care program to be accomplished by restructuring of the financing mechanism for health services delivery.[22] Others argue that problems in the financing mechanism are only symptoms of the disease and that the real problems are in the structure of the health delivery system itself. For example, Garfield states that national health insurance will only aggravate the problems related to health services in the United States.[23] He contends that the increased demands for services which would result from extension of health insurance to the entire population of the United States would only result in serious deterioration in the quality and availability of health services for the sick.

Paul Cornely is concerned that proposals for national health insurance ignore preventive health measures. In an editorial entitled, "There is More to Health than Just Paying Bills," he states:

> It would be hoped also that all branches of our government would become responsive to factors of health rather than focusing only on the cure of disease or the economics involved . . . But if any of the present bills or any compromises of them are passed, they will simply perpetuate the present

[21] Anne R. Somers, *Health Care in Transition: Directions for the Future* (Chicago: Hospital Research and Educational Trust, 1971), pp. 39–72.

[22] Isidores S. Falk, *National Policies and Programs for Financing of Medical Care*, The 1971 Michael M. Davis Lecture (Chicago: Center for Health Administration Studies, University of Chicago, 1971).

[23] Sidney R. Garfield, "The Delivery of Medical Care," *Scientific American* 222 (April, 1970): 15–23.

system of just treating and caring for those who are sick, disabled, or dying. They do not address the larger and obvious challenge of preventing health problems.[24]

McNerney presents a detailed analysis of the problems associated with the cost of medical care.[25] He is not bothered by the fact that the increasing demand for services has contributed to the rapid rise in cost. However, he points out that the institutional and financial arrangements by which services are rendered are badly out of date, and the resultant inefficiencies and excess costs represent problems which must be dealt with effectively. He points out that many of the problems relate to health manpower and its poor distribution among the populace. He contends that more than 60 percent of health care costs are attributable directly to manpower which must become the prime target for reform if health care costs are to be moderated.

This study focuses most of its attention on the effects of health care costs on the consumer sector of the population, an area in which very few studies could be found in the literature.

Kenneth Boulding discusses the much debated question of need versus demand for health services.[26] He points out that if real needs are to be well satisfied, then demand must be stimulated to some extent. In the case of medical indigency, he warns against the temptation to deny consumer sovereignty as the price for the relief of indigency—to say that the poor must have what the professionals think is good for them in this situation.

Kindig and Sidel describe a set of criteria for measuring the impact of proposed national health insurance programs on the consumer.[27] The criteria seem to be overly simplistic and do not

[24] Paul B. Cornely, "There is More to Health than Just Paying Bills," *American Journal of Public Health* 64 (September, 1974): 917.

[25] Walter J. McNerney, "Why Does Medical Care Cost So Much?," *New England Journal of Medicine* 282 (June, 1970): 1458–65.

[26] Kenneth E. Boulding, "The Concept of Need for Health Services," *Milbank Memorial Fund Quarterly* XLIV (October, 1966): 202–21.

[27] David A. Kindig and Victor W. Sidel, "Proposed National Health Insurance Programs: Impact on the Consumer" (paper delivered at the National Health Insurance Conference at the University of Pennsylvania, Philadelphia, November 12–13, 1970).

appear to be based upon substantive evidence resulting from empirical studies, a characteristic of many similar criteria which are now proliferating in the literature.

Some of the most detailed and careful work dealing with the impact of health costs on the consumer has been carried out by Martin Feldstein. In discussing the rapid increases in the cost of hospital care, he explodes several myths. In comparison with the prices of other goods or services that the household buys, the cost of medical care has not changed very much over the last few years. Furthermore, the consumer is buying a better and more sophisticated product than he did a few years back.

> Now, in terms of net cost, income has been rising rather rapidly. It used to take seven hours of work to buy a day's care (hospital care). By 1968 that was down to five and a half.[28]

Feldstein also points out that the inability of consumers to pay for their own hospital care is not the essence of the problem. Rather, the challenge to government policy is to restructure forms of health insurance so that the future development of hospital care will be more truly responsive to the preferences of the consumer, rather than being determined by the providers and third party payors as they are today.

The popular press has recently published a large number of articles which discuss the "crisis" in health care in the United States. Articles in periodicals such as *Saturday Review*, *Fortune*, the weekly news magazines, and newspapers throughout the country decry the problems of rising health care costs. With varying degrees of objectivity, they have presented the problems of the United States health care system to their readers.[29]

[28] Martin S. Feldstein, "Today's Hospital Costs—What Produced Them?," *Massachusetts Hospital Association Newsletter Supplement* (September, 1971): 6–11.

[29] See, for example: Abraham Ribicoff, "Health Care: Rx for Change—The 'Healthiest Nation' Myth," *Saturday Review*, 22 August 1970, p. 18–20; "Behind the Rising Cost of Health Care," *U.S. News and World Report*, 16 March 1970, p. 63; "Mr. Nixon's Health Care Plan," *Newsweek*, 1 March 1971; "Our Ailing Medical System: It's Time to Operate," *Fortune*, January, 1970, pp. 78–79.

These popular articles also present convincing evidence that the movement toward a national health policy is indeed becoming an important political issue in the United States. An article in *Time* magazine presents a good summary of the political realities involved:

> The problems are numerous and complex, including the training of medical personnel, the organization of hospitals and the melding of private and public facilities. But public attention has focused most sharply on the price of visiting a doctor's office or staying in a hospital. Politics is following that preoccupation. Republicans and Democrats, liberals and conservatives, and even the American Medical Association, which fought Medicare for so long, are all agreed that a new federal role is necessary to help Americans pay their bills . . . It will be the rare candidate in 1972 who will feel comfortable without having voted aye (for some form of national health insurance).[30]

A recent article in the *New York Times Magazine* reinforces this theme of the growing importance of health in the political scene and the inevitable passage of national health insurance legislation in the near future.[31] The article points out that a recent legislative rush has been towards national health insurance and that even the leaders of the American Medical Association overwhelmingly believe that some form of national health insurance will be enacted. The article also includes a detailed examination of current legislative proposals and comments on their likelihood of passage. The *Cincinnati Enquirer* states that the debate over national health insurance will represent one of the most significant legislative struggles in American history.[32]

In the preceding review of the literature, several important patterns of analysis for this study have emerged. First, most policy-making in this country has been carried out on an incremental basis, with one decision building on another, and with minimum employment of detailed data analysis to support policy decisions. In short,

[30] "Health Care: Supply, Demand and Politics," *Time*, 7 June 1971, pp. 86–93.

[31] Alice M. Rivlin, "Agreed: Here Comes National Health Insurance, Question: What Kind?" *New York Times Magazine*, 21 July 1974.

[32] Robert Webb, "Health Plans Flood Senate Hoppers," *Cincinnati Enquirer*, 9 May 1971.

policy-making is largely a process of competing political advocacy by various special interest groups. The results of the advocacy process tend to be only small shifts from current policies. In observing the above, political scientists are agreed that the incremental, special-interest approach is descriptive of most current policy decisions. Many of them believe, however, that this "nonplanning" process cannot continue to be employed with the problems of our society growing ever more complex.

Second, the delivery of health services is an issue of growing political importance in this country. Problems in our present system of health care, particularly rapidly rising costs and uneven distribution of services, are receiving growing attention in the popular press. There seems to be general agreement that our first major attack on these problems will be the passage of some form of national health insurance in the not-too-distant future.

A critical question is thus posed. Will the debate over national health insurance become just another example of the political advocacy process, or will major decisions be reached through a more careful process of data collection and analysis? The remainder of this study attempts to answer this question by examining one aspect of the debate in its early stages.

STUDY METHODOLOGY 2

Objectives of the Research and Plan for the Study

In order to test the extent to which the debate about national health insurance is based on rational analysis of data, this research project focuses on one important aspect of the health care system, the costs of health services to the consumer.

In order to establish a base for comparative purposes, an economic model was established which describes consumer spending patterns for a twenty-two year period, post-World War II, from 1948 to 1969. From this model, a set of data elements were enumerated which are critical for accurate description of consumer spending patterns for health care. The development of this economic model is described in Chapter 3.

Five major proposals for national health insurance which were introduced into Congress during 1971 provide the basis for comparison. Background data in support of each of these proposals were obtained and special analysis of economic data was carried out. The critical data elements developed from the author's economic model were compared to economic indicators found in the background documentation of the five major health insurance proposals to see how well these proposals have accurately described consumer spending patterns for health services. This comparative analysis is discussed in Chapter 4.

Hence, the analysis addresses two major questions:

(1) Whether data on consumer health expenditures are being accurately presented by those submitting plans for national health insurance, and

(2) Whether the proposals are being supported by sound data analysis, or whether they are based primarily on the hidden agendas of the special interest groups involved.

The research for this study was completed in 1971. Since that time some modifications have occurred in the leading national health insurance proposals. However, the five proposals reviewed in 1971 are still typical of the kinds of proposals being debated in Congress in 1975, and the validity of the comparisons should not be hampered by the passage of time. In order to insure that the economic model has not changed substantially, the author obtained additional data for 1970 through 1972 and found that the regressions remained essentially unchanged.

Data Sources

The data used in this study were obtained from two departments of the federal government, the Department of Health, Education and Welfare and the Department of Commerce. Table 1 is a glossary of data elements, including the symbol, definition, and source for each data element used in the analysis.

General economic data were obtained from Department of Commerce publications as indicated in Table 1. These data elements include Gross National Product, Disposable Personal Income, Total Personal Consumption Expenditures, and Implicit Price Deflators for converting general economic data into a constant dollar base. Note that the base year for the price deflators is 1958, halfway through the twenty-two year time period which the study covers.

One other source of general economic data was utilized. During the study I examined the relationship of Consumer Expenditures for Personal Health Care to expenditures from Discretionary Income. Discretionary Income is that income over which consumers can exercise some independent choice as to spending or saving, i.e., income available after fixed contractual commitments each month have been paid. These data were obtained from the National Consumer Finance Association through their *Finance Facts Yearbooks* for 1969, 1970, and 1971.

Health economic data were obtained from the Office of Research and Statistics, Social Security Administration of the Department of Health, Education and Welfare. These data tables provided information on national expenditures for personal health care, a breakout into public and private expenditures, and a further breakout into consumer expenditures for personal health care including the cost of health insurance premiums. In addition, the *Social Security Bulletin* of April, 1971, was used to obtain data on expenditures for Medicare and Medicaid (note that the Medicaid data include expenditures under a pre-Medicare Social Security Administration program of Medical Assistance for the Aged).

The data obtained from these tables were the very latest available and include corrections and adjustments to data previously published in the *Social Security Bulletin.* The basic data as described above are included in three tables: Table 2, General Economic Data; Table 3, Health Economic Data; and Table 4, Implicit Price Deflators.

Data Processing and Tabulation Procedures

The Xavier University Computer Center (Cincinnati, Ohio) was utilized for tabulation and statistical analysis of data. Six computer programs were written by the author to organize and display the data and compute basic ratios. In addition, statistical library programs were used for curve-fitting of the time-trend data. These programs were also used for correlation analysis between variables

Table 1

GLOSSARY OF SYMBOLS FOR DATA ELEMENTS USED IN THE STUDY

Symbol	Data Element and Definition	Source of Data
GNP	*Gross National Product.* The market value of the output of goods and services produced by the Nation's economy.	U.S. Dept. of Commerce: 1. *The National Income and Product Accounts of the United States 1929–1965* Statistical Tables
DPI	*Disposable Personal Income.* The income remaining to persons after payment of personal taxes.	
TCE	*Total Personal Consumption Expenditures.* The market value of goods and services purchased by individuals and non-profit institutions or acquired by them as income in kind.	2. *Survey of Current Business*, Vol. 50, No. 7, July 1970
DGNP	*Implicit Price Deflator for Gross National Product.* A weighted average of the price indexes used to deflate the components of GNP. Base year for all implicit price deflators is 1958.	
DDPI	*Implicit Price Deflator for Disposable Personal Income,* Total Personal Consumption Expenditures, and Expenditures from Discretionary Income.	
DME	*Implicit Price Deflator* for all personal health care expenditure data	
CDI	*Expenditures from Discretionary Income.* Expenditures made from income over which consumers exercise independent choice as to spending or saving (after fixed contractual commitments have been paid).	National Consumer Finance Association, *Finance Facts Yearbooks* for 1971, 1970, 1969.
TME	*Total National Expenditures for Personal Health Care.* All expenditures for health services and supplies other than (1) expenses for prepayment and administration, (2) Government public health activities, and (3) expenditures of private voluntary agencies for other health services.	U.S. Dept. of Health, Education and Welfare, Social Security Administration, Office of Research and Statistics. Data tables

Symbol	Data Element and Definition	Source of Data
PUME	*Total Public Expenditures for Personal Health Care.* Paid by Government agencies; federal, state, and local.	
PRME	*Total Private Expenditures for Personal Health Care.* Paid by individuals or non-governmental organizations.	
CEM	*Consumer Expenditures for Personal Health Care.* Includes the cost of health insurance premiums.	
EMC	*Expenditures for Medicare.* Federal expenditures under the program of health insurance for those age 65 and over.	*Social Security Bulletin*—April 1971
EMD	*Expenditures for Medicaid and Medical Assistance for the Aged.* Federal expenditures under Title 19 of the Medicare Act and a previous Social Security Program of Medical Assistance for the Aged.	

NOTE: Any symbol with a C (exception EMC) as the last letter refers to that variable in Constant (1958) Dollars—i.e., with the appropriate implicit price deflator applied.

and for an analysis of variance to test for goodness of fit of the time-trend curves. All programs were written in FORTRAN IV language for the IBM 360 Disc Operating System. The six programs written by the author are included as an Appendix.

Analytical Procedures

This study focuses on an examination of relative economic data. Data on expenditures for personal health care are examined as relative measures to general economic statistics. For this reason, the first part of the analysis involved the computation of various ratios such as the ratio of Consumer Expenditures for Personal Health

TABLE 2

GENERAL ECONOMIC DATA
(All Dollar Figures in Billions)

Year	Gross National Product (GNP) [1 2]	Disposable Personal Income (DPI) [1 2]	Total Personal Consumption Expenditures (TCE) [1 2]	Expenditures from Discretionary Income (CDI) [3]
1948	$257.600	$189.138	$173.555	—
1949	256.500	188.585	176.803	—
1950	284.800	206.940	191.009	—
1951	328.400	226.583	206.266	—
1952	345.500	238.312	216.679	—
1953	364.600	252.564	229.969	—
1954	364.800	257.445	236.494	—
1955	398.000	275.348	254.381	—
1956	419.200	293.179	266.675	—
1957	441.100	308.524	281.432	—
1958	447.300	318.826	290.069	—
1959	483.700	337.315	311.207	$129.900
1960	503.700	350.044	325.241	130.600
1961	520.100	364.424	335.152	133.400
1962	560.300	385.267	355.057	141.800
1963	590.500	404.604	374.982	149.400
1964	632.400	438.100	401.200	165.400
1965	684.900	473.200	432.800	175.200
1966	749.900	511.852	466.334	190.400
1967	793.900	546.341	492.066	194.800
1968	865.000	591.199	535.834	225.200
1969	931.400	631.569	577.458	239.800

SOURCE: [1] U.S. Dept. of Commerce: *The National Income and Product Accounts of the United States 1929–1965* Statistical Tables.
[2] U.S. Dept. of Commerce: *Survey of Current Business*, Vol. 50, No. 7, July 1970.
[3] National Consumer Finance Association. *Finance Facts Yearbooks* for 1971, 1970, 1969.

TABLE 3

HEALTH ECONOMIC DATA
(All Dollar Figures in Billions)

Year	Total National Expenditures For Personal Health Care (TME)[1]	Total Public Expenditures for Personal Health Care (PUME)[1]	Total Private Expenditures for Personal Health Care (PRME)[1]	Consumer Expenditures for Personal Health Care (CEM)[1]	Expenditures for Medicare (EMC)[2]	Expenditures for Medicaid and Medical Assistance for the Aged (EMD)[2]
1948	$ 9.473	$ 1.779	$ 7.694	$ 7.435	$0.0	$0.0
1949	10.073	1.995	8.078	7.793	0.0	0.0
1950	10.909	2.440	8.469	8.149	0.0	0.0
1951	12.102	3.035	9.067	8.725	0.0	0.0
1952	13.047	3.307	9.740	9.379	0.0	0.0
1953	13.916	3.335	10.581	10.199	0.0	0.0
1954	14.853	3.410	11.443	11.030	0.0	0.0
1955	15.740	3.608	12.132	11.700	0.0	0.0
1956	17.177	3.919	13.258	12.802	0.0	0.0
1957	18.637	4.234	14.403	13.923	0.0	0.0
1958	20.247	4.532	15.715	15.213	0.0	0.0
1959	22.032	4.808	17.224	16.672	0.0	0.0
1960	23.758	5.157	18.603	18.066	0.0	0.005
1961	25.184	5.578	19.608	19.031	0.0	0.113
1962	27.131	5.967	21.163	20.555	0.0	0.251
1963	29.088	6.419	22.669	22.028	0.0	0.329
1964	32.408	6.904	25.505	24.837	0.0	0.445
1965	34.942	7.345	27.599	26.902	0.0	0.586
1966	38.794	9.534	29.260	28.516	1.019	1.487
1967	44.037	14.591	29.447	28.682	4.550	2.574
1968	49.207	17.487	31.719	30.929	5.697	3.848
1969	55.296	19.520	35.778	34.939	6.604	4.419

SOURCE: [1] U.S. Dept. of Health, Education, and Welfare, Social Security Administration, Office of Research and Statistics. Data tables—pre-publication.
[2] *Social Security Bulletin*—April 1971

Care to Disposable Personal Income. The computer programs written by the author produced these ratios which are discussed in the next chapter. In addition, the ratios were recomputed after price effect had been removed by applying the appropriate Implicit Price Deflator to each of the data elements. Thus the ratios can be compared in current dollars and in constant dollars with price effect removed.

The next portion of the analysis involved the fitting of time-trend lines and curves to several of the variables, and also the analysis of

TABLE 4

IMPLICIT PRICE DEFLATORS

Year	Deflator for Gross National Product	Deflator for Disposable Personal Income, Personal Consumption Expenditures, and Expenditures from Discretionary Income	Deflator for Personal Health Care Expenditures
1948	79.6%	82.3%	73.1%
1949	79.1	81.7	73.2
1950	80.2	82.9	74.2
1951	85.6	88.6	76.0
1952	87.5	90.5	80.2
1953	88.3	91.7	84.9
1954	89.6	92.5	88.4
1955	90.9	92.8	91.0
1956	94.0	94.8	92.9
1957	97.5	97.7	96.6
1958	100.0	100.0	100.0
1959	101.6	101.3	103.8
1960	103.3	102.9	108.0
1961	104.6	103.9	111.2
1962	105.8	104.9	115.0
1963	107.2	106.1	117.7
1964	108.9	107.4	121.4
1965	110.9	108.9	124.5
1966	113.9	111.5	132.4
1967	117.6	114.4	142.3
1968	122.3	118.5	150.5
1969	128.1	123.5	161.7

SOURCE: U.S. Dept. of Commerce: *The National Income and Product Accounts of the United States 1929–1965* Statistical Tables.
U.S. Dept. of Commerce: *Survey of Current Business*, Vol. 50, No. 7 July 1970

the relationship between these variables using correlation coefficients and an analysis of variance.[1]

Using the least-squares method, each of the variable sets were fitted to a time-trend line using three different functions: a simple linear function of the form $y=a+bx$, a log transformation of the linear function, and a quadratic function of the form $y=ax^2+bx+c$. In addition, consumer data relative to general economic measures were separated into the pre- and post-Medicare periods, using a technique involving dummy variables.[2] The closeness of the association between variables was measured by means of the correlation coefficient and the standard error of the coefficient. Correlation coefficients were corrected for small samples.[3]

In order to remove some of the time dependence from the data, first differences were computed for Consumer Expenditures for Personal Health Care and Disposable Personal Income. First differences are obtained by subtracting the value of the variable in a given year (year n) from the value of that same variable in the following year (n+1), i.e., computing the differences from year to year. Time-trend analysis was also carried out using these first differences.

The third major portion of the analysis was the comparison of these relative economic statistics with supporting economic data for various proposals for national health insurance being offered by several special interest groups in the health field. A comprehensive review of supporting material for these proposals was conducted, and comparative analysis was made with the following proposals introduced into Congress during 1971.

1. The proposal by organized labor and the Committee for National Health Insurance, introduced into Congress by Senator Edward M. Kennedy and Representative Martha W. Griffiths;

[1] Edward J. Kane, *Economic Statistics and Econometrics* (New York: Harper & Row, Inc., 1968), chapters 10 and 12, and James S. Duesenberry, "Income-Consumption Relations and Their Implications," in *Macroeconomic Readings*, John Lindauer, ed. (New York: The Free Press, 1968).

[2] J. Johnston, *Econometric Methods* (New York: McGraw-Hill Book Co., 1963), pp. 221–228.

[3] Michael J. Brennan, *Preface to Econometrics* (Cincinnati, Ohio: Southwestern Publishing Co., 1965), pp. 315–318.

2. the American Medical Association proposal entitled Medicredit;
3. the American Hospital Association proposal called Ameriplan;
4. the private health insurance industry proposal entitled Healthcare; and
5. the Nixon Administration proposal for a national health insurance partnership.

In addition, the ten-volume set of Sub-committee Hearings produced by Senator Kennedy's Senate Subcommittee on Health were reviewed to see what types of economic data were used by the many interest groups who testified before that Subcommittee in the Spring and Summer of 1971.

Study Limitations

The use of aggregated data which is time-related from year to year constitutes one limitation to this study. Robinson calls this the problem of ecological correlations.[4] Ecological correlation is the development of a relationship between aggregate measures of phenomena that tend to move together or are naturally correlated. Robinson points out that ecological correlations are used simply because correlations between the properties of individuals are not available. Clearly, disaggregate data are preferable to aggregate data, but when they are not available (as is the case in this study), then we must work with aggregated data recognizing the limitations of it. Since this study is concerned with a macro-examination of U.S. health expenditures in order to examine national policy, the use of aggregated data is necessary and appropriate.

A second major limitation relates to the comparative analysis of economic statistics used by political advocates promoting their proposals for national health policy and national health insurance. Keeping up-to-date with the rapidly changing picture on national health insurance is problematic; however, this study attempts to carry out the analysis at a fixed point in time, although before the

[4] W. S. Robinson, "Ecological Correlations and the Behavior of Individuals," *American Sociological Review* 15 (1950): 351–7.

results are published, other changes will have occurred. It appears that the primary structure of the proposals have now been fairly well established, and major changes to them are not expected. For this reason, the comparative analysis should have validity over time.

AN ECONOMIC MODEL OF EXPENDITURES FOR HEALTH CARE 3

Little attention is given in medical care literature to the consumer and the effects of health costs on the consumer sector of the economy. Even more unusual is the examination of consumer expenditures for personal health care in relative terms, i.e., spending relative to income. A paper by Martin Feldstein represents one notable exception.[1] Feldstein points out that the number of hours the consumer must work to pay for a day of hospital care has decreased since World War II, a fact largely ignored in the literature. Relative spending for health care is examined in more detail in this chapter.

Consumer Expenditures for Personal Health Care and Disposable Personal Income

Table 5 presents a set of ratios of Consumer Expenditures for Personal Health Care to Disposable Personal Income in current dollars and constant dollars for the twenty-two-year period from 1948 to 1969.

[1] Feldstein, "Today's Hospital Costs—What Produced Them?," pp. 6–11.

TABLE 5

CONSUMER EXPENDITURES FOR PERSONAL HEALTH CARE
AS A PERCENTAGE OF DISPOSABLE PERSONAL INCOME
(All Dollar Figures in Billions)

Year	In current dollars			In constant dollars		
	Consumer Expenditures for Personal Health Care (CEM)[1]	Disposable Personal Income (DPI)[2]	CEM/DPI	Consumer Expenditures for Personal Health Care (CEMC)[1]	Disposable Personal Income (DPIC)[2]	CEMC/DPIC
1948	$ 7.435	$189.138	3.9%	$10.171	$229.815	4.4%
1949	7.793	188.585	4.1	10.646	230.826	4.6
1950	8.149	206.940	3.9	10.982	249.626	4.4
1951	8.725	226.583	3.9	11.480	255.737	4.5
1952	9.379	238.312	3.9	11.695	263.328	4.4
1953	10.199	252.564	4.0	12.013	275.424	4.4
1954	11.030	257.445	4.3	12.477	278.319	4.5
1955	11.700	275.348	4.2	12.857	296.711	4.3
1956	12.802	293.179	4.4	13.780	309.260	4.5
1957	13.923	308.524	4.5	14.413	315.787	4.6
1958	15.213	318.826	4.8	15.213	318.826	4.8
1959	16.672	337.315	4.9	16.062	332.986	4.8
1960	18.066	350.044	5.2	16.728	340.179	4.9
1961	19.031	364.424	5.2	17.114	350.745	4.9
1962	20.555	385.267	5.3	17.874	367.271	4.9
1963	22.028	404.604	5.4	18.715	381.342	4.9
1964	24.837	438.100	5.7	20.459	407.914	5.0
1965	26.902	473.200	5.7	21.608	434.926	5.0
1966	28.516	511.852	5.6	21.538	459.060	4.7
1967	28.682	546.341	5.2	20.156	477.571	4.2
1968	30.929	591.199	5.2	20.551	498.902	4.1
1969	34.939	631.569	5.5	21.607	511.392	4.2

SOURCE: [1] U.S. Dept. of Health, Education and Welfare, Social Security Administration, Office of Research and Statistics. Data tables—pre-publication.
[2] U.S. Dept. of Commerce: *The National Income and Product Accounts of the United States 1929–1965* Statistical Tables
U.S. Dept. of Commerce: *Survey of Current Business*, Vol. 50, No. 7 July 1970

In current dollar terms, the ratio increased from 3.9 percent to 5.5 percent during this time period. However, in real terms with price effect removed, the ratio decreased from 4.4 percent in 1948 to 4.2 percent in 1969. This is shown graphically in Figure 1.

From these ratios, it can be seen that if medical prices were brought in line with other prices of goods and services to consumers, then the consumer would be spending a *fixed percentage* of his income for personal health care, not the dramatic increases in spending which we hear so much about in the contemporary medical care literature.

CONSUMER EXPENDITURES FOR PERSONAL HEALTH CARE
AS A PERCENTAGE OF DISPOSABLE PERSONAL INCOME
1948–1969

(All Dollar Figures in Billions)

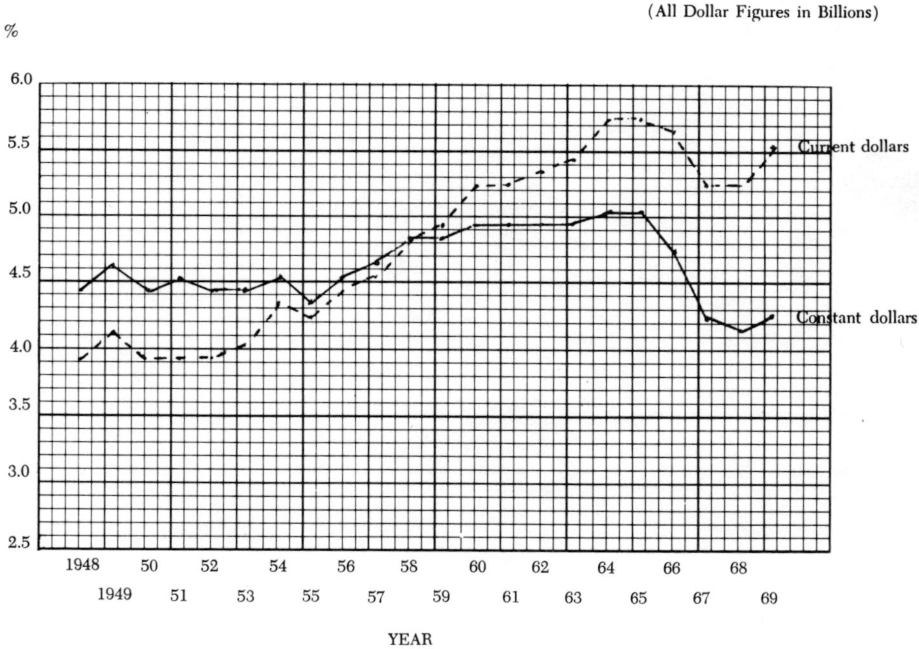

FIGURE 1

Statistical verification of these findings was obtained by fitting trend lines to the data and computing correlation coefficients, the results of which are shown in Table 6. The variables were related with three different functions: a simple linear function, a logarithmic transformation of the linear function, and a quadratic function. Highly significant associations between the variables were obtained in all cases, in both current and constant dollar terms. Statistical significance was tested by means of the r^2 value and the standard error of the coefficient, both of which are also shown in Table 6. The best r^2 value was obtained by fitting the quadratic function.

TABLE 6

Correlation Analysis
CONSUMER EXPENDITURES FOR PERSONAL HEALTH CARE AND DISPOSABLE PERSONAL INCOME

Variable 1 (Y)	Variable 2 (X)	Line (Curve) of Best Fit	r^2 Raw	r^2 Corrected for Small Sample	Standard Error of Coefficient
CEM (Current Dollars)	DPI	1. $Y = -5.12 + 0.064X$	0.986	0.985	0.0017
		2. $Y = -8.66 + 0.084X - 0.000026X^2$	0.989	0.988	0.010 0.000012
		3. $\text{Log } Y = -5.07 + 1.35 \text{ Log } X$	0.986	0.985	0.036
CEMC (Constant Dollars)	DPIC	1. $Y = 0.64 + 0.044X$	0.926	0.919	0.0028
		2. $Y = -14.28 + 0.13X - 0.00012X^2$	0.966	0.963	0.018 0.000025
		3. $\text{Log } Y = -3.15 + 1.01 \text{ Log } X$	0.948	0.943	0.053

CEM = Consumer Expenditures for Personal Health Care.
DPI = Disposable Personal Income.

Time Period: 1948–1969

To summarize this portion of the analysis, Consumer Expenditures for Personal Health Care and Disposable Personal Income appear to be closely related. When price effect is removed, the consumer spends a fixed portion of his income for personal health care.

Consumer Expenditures for Personal Health Care and Total Personal Consumption Expenditures.

The same type of analysis was repeated using Total Personal Consumption Expenditures rather than Disposable Personal Income as the independent variable. This eliminates consumer savings, and the analysis deals totally with actual consumption expenditures.

Table 7 shows the ratios of Consumer Expenditures for Personal

TABLE 7

CONSUMER EXPENDITURES FOR PERSONAL HEALTH CARE AS A PERCENTAGE OF TOTAL PERSONAL CONSUMPTION EXPENDITURES
(All Dollar Figures in Billions)

Year	In current dollars			In constant dollars		
	Consumer Expenditures for Personal Health Care (CEM)[1]	Total Personal Consumption Expenditures (TCE)[2]	CEM/TCE	Consumer Expenditures for Personal Health Care (CEMC)[1]	Total Personal Consumption Expenditures (TCEC)[2]	CEMC/TCEC
1948	$ 7.435	$173.555	4.3%	$10.171	$210.881	4.8%
1949	7.793	176.803	4.4	10.646	216.405	4.9
1950	8.149	191.009	4.3	10.982	230.409	4.8
1951	8.725	206.266	4.2	11.480	232.806	4.9
1952	9.379	216.679	4.3	11.695	239.424	4.9
1953	10.199	229.969	4.4	12.013	250.784	4.8
1954	11.030	236.494	4.7	12.477	255.669	4.9
1955	11.700	254.381	4.6	12.857	274.117	4.7
1956	12.802	266.675	4.8	13.780	281.302	4.9
1957	13.923	281.432	4.9	14.413	288.057	5.0
1958	15.213	290.069	5.2	15.213	290.069	5.2
1959	16.672	311.207	5.4	16.062	307.213	5.2
1960	18.066	325.241	5.6	16.728	316.075	5.3
1961	19.031	335.152	5.7	17.114	322.572	5.3
1962	20.555	355.057	5.8	17.874	338.472	5.3
1963	22.028	374.982	5.9	18.715	353.423	5.3
1964	24.837	401.200	6.2	20.459	373.557	5.5
1965	26.902	432.800	6.2	21.608	397.428	5.4
1966	28.516	466.334	6.1	21.538	418.237	5.1
1967	28.682	492.066	5.8	20.156	430.127	4.7
1968	30.929	535.834	5.8	20.551	452.180	4.5
1969	34.939	577.458	6.1	21.607	467.577	4.6

SOURCE: [1] U.S. Dept. of Health, Education and Welfare, Social Security Administration, Office of Research and Statistics. Data tables—pre-publication.
[2] U.S. Dept. of Commerce: *The National Income and Product Accounts of the United States 1929–1965 Statistical* Tables.
Survey of Current Business, Vol. 50, No. 7 July 1970

Health Care to Total Personal Consumption Expenditures in both current and constant dollars for the period 1948 through 1969.

A similar pattern to that of Disposable Personal Income is observed. In current dollars or non-deflated terms, the ratio increased from 4.3 percent to 6.1 percent over the twenty-two-year span.

However, in constant dollar terms, the ratio decreased slightly from 4.8 percent to 4.6 percent. This is shown graphically in Figure 2.

Again, in real terms, the consumer spends a fixed percentage of his overall consumption expenditures for personal health care items.

A correlation analysis was also made of Consumer Expenditures for Personal Health Care and Total Personal Consumption Expenditures with the results shown in Table 8. Once again three functions were fitted to the data in both current and constant dollar terms: a linear function, a logarithmic transformation, and a quadratic function. As with Disposable Personal Income, highly significant associations for all three of these functions were obtained in both current and constant dollars. However, as indicated by the r^2 value, a slightly better fit was obtained using the quadratic function.

Consumer Expenditures for Personal Health Care and Discretionary Income

In order to further examine the income elasticity of Consumer Expenditures for Personal Health Care, ratios to Discretionary Income were computed. Discretionary Income is the income available to consumers after fixed monthly commitments (for example, house payments and car payments) are paid. It is income over which consumers can exercise some spending or non-spending options.

Table 9 shows these ratios for the eleven-year period from 1959 to 1969 in both current and constant dollars. Note that data from 1948 through 1958 on Discretionary Income were not available and hence could not be used in the analysis.

In examining discretionary spending patterns, we see an even more dramatic example of fixed percentage spending for personal health care. In current dollars, the percentage increased very slightly from 12.8 percent to 14.6 percent over the eleven-year period. However, in constant dollars it decreased from 12.5 percent in 1959 to 11.1 percent in 1969.

A correlation analysis relating Consumer Expenditures for Personal Health Care and Discretionary Income was carried out using the linear function only, since very little difference was found in the previous analyses in utilizing other transformations. The results of

CONSUMER EXPENDITURES FOR PERSONAL HEALTH CARE
AS A PERCENTAGE OF TOTAL PERSONAL CONSUMPTION
EXPENDITURES 1948–1969

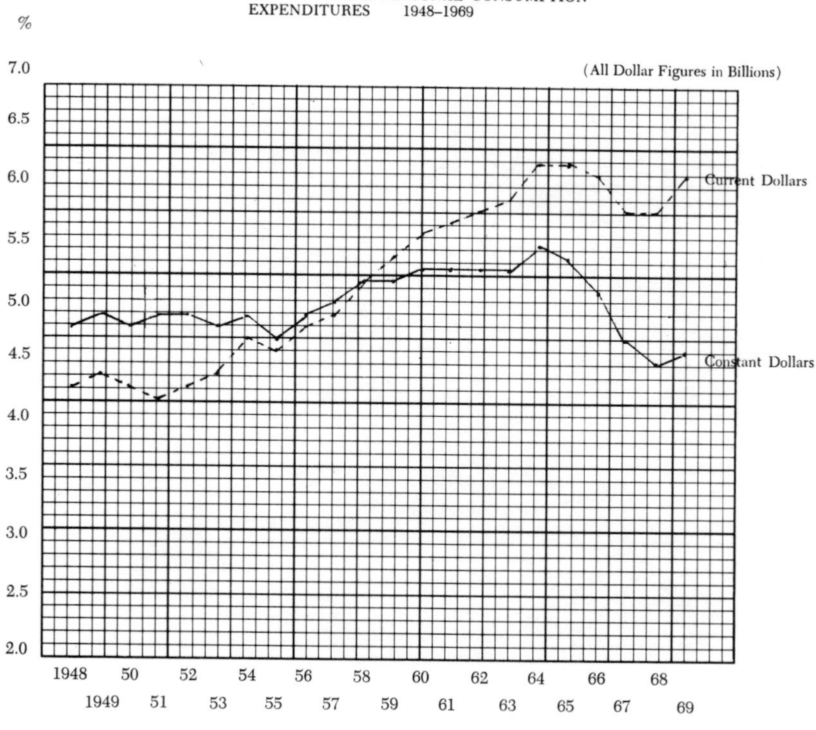

FIGURE 2

TABLE 8

Correlation Analysis
CONSUMER EXPENDITURES FOR PERSONAL HEALTH CARE AND TOTAL PERSONAL CONSUMPTION EXPENDITURES

Variable 1 (Y)	Variable 2 (X)	Line (Curve) of Best Fit	r^2 Raw	r^2 Corrected for Small Sample	Standard Error of Coefficient
CEM (Current Dollars)	TCE	1. $Y = -5.41 + 0.071X$	0.989	0.988	0.0016
		2. $Y = -8.49 + 0.09X - 0.000027X^2$	0.991	0.990	0.0098 0.000013
		3. $\text{Log } Y = -5.04 + 1.36 \text{ Log } X$	0.989	0.988	0.032
CEMC (Constant Dollars)	TCEC	1. $Y = 0.32 + 0.049X$	0.934	0.927	0.0029
		2. $Y = -14.20 + 0.14X - 0.00014X^2$	0.970	0.967	0.019 0.000029
		3. $\text{Log } Y = -3.17 + 1.03 \text{ Log } X$	0.955	0.951	0.05

CEM = Consumer Expenditures for Personal Health Care.
TCE = Total Personal Consumption Expenditures.
Time Period: 1948–1969

TABLE 9

CONSUMER EXPENDITURES FOR PERSONAL HEALTH CARE AS A PERCENTAGE OF EXPENDITURES FROM DISCRETIONARY INCOME
(All Dollar Figures in Billions)

Year	In current dollars: Consumer Expenditures for Personal Health Care (CEM) [1]	Expenditures from Discretionary Income (CDI) [2]	CEM / CDI	In constant dollars: Consumer Expenditures for Personal Health Care (CEMC) [1]	Expenditures from Discretionary Income (CDIC) [2]	CEMC / CDIC
1959	$16.672	$129.900	12.8%	$16.062	$128.233	12.5%
1960	18.066	130.600	13.8	16.728	126.919	13.2
1961	19.031	133.400	14.3	17.114	128.393	13.3
1962	20.555	141.800	14.5	17.874	135.176	13.2
1963	22.028	149.400	14.7	18.715	140.811	13.3
1964	24.837	165.400	15.0	20.459	154.004	13.3
1965	26.902	175.200	15.4	21.608	161.029	13.4
1966	28.516	190.400	15.0	21.538	170.762	12.6
1967	28.682	194.800	14.7	20.156	170.280	11.8
1968	30.929	225.200	13.7	20.551	190.042	10.8
1969	34.939	239.800	14.6	21.607	194.170	11.1

SOURCE: [1] U.S. Dept. of Health, Education and Welfare, Social Security Administration, Office of Research and Statistics. Data tables—pre-publication.

[2] National Consumer Finance Association. *Finance Facts Yearbooks* for 1971, 1970, 1969

this correlation analysis are shown in Table 10. Once again a highly significant r^2 value and standard error of the coefficient were obtained, showing strong association between the variables in both current and constant dollar terms.

TABLE 10

Correlation Analysis
CONSUMER EXPENDITURES FOR PERSONAL HEALTH CARE AND CONSUMER EXPENDITURES FROM DISCRETIONARY INCOME

Variable 1 (Y)	Variable 2 (X)	Line (Curve) of Best Fit	r^2 Raw	r^2 Corrected for Small Sample	Standard Error of Coefficient
CEM (Current Dollars)	CDI	Y = −0.95 + 0.15X	0.964	0.956	0.0096
CEMC (Constant Dollars)	CDIC	Y = 7.91 + 0.074X	0.761	0.708	0.0138

CEM = Consumer Expenditures for Personal Health Care.
CDI = Expenditures from Discretionary Income.
Time Period: 1959–1969

Thus we again see that Consumer Expenditures for Personal Health Care appear to be directly related to the amount of *spendable* income available to consumers after their fixed monthly contractual commitments have been paid.

Pre- and Post-Medicare Differences

Since the quadratic function seemed to give the best fit of the variables in the previous analyses, and since the data seemed to contain the most curvature (with decreasing slope) during the last four or five years, it was decided to fit two linear functions to the data: one for the pre-Medicare era from 1948 to 1965 and the other for the post-Medicare period from 1966 to 1969.

Dummy variables were used to fit double functions under two separate assumptions. Under assumption 1, the slopes were assumed to be the same but the two functions would have different intercepts, i.e., they would constitute two parallel lines. For assumption 2, both the slopes and intercepts were assumed to be different so that two non-parallel lines would represent pre- and post-Medicare periods.[2]

The results of this analysis are shown in Table 11. Once again,

TABLE 11

Correlation Analysis
SEPARATION OF PRE-MEDICARE AND POST-MEDICARE ERAS

ASSUMPTION 1: Common Slope; Different Intercepts (Parallel Lines)

Variable 1 (Y)	Variable 2 (X)	Line of Best Fit [1]	r^2 Raw	r^2 Corrected for Small Sample
CEM	DPI	$Y = -9.21 + 2.45X_2 + 0.07X$	0.991	0.990
CEMC	DPIC	$Y = -6.53 + 3.52X_2 + 0.056X$	0.972	0.969
CEM	TCE	$Y = -8.76 + 1.20X_2 + 0.076X$	0.993	0.992
CEMC	TCEC	$Y = -6.27 + 3.23X_2 + 0.062X$	0.975	0.973

ASSUMPTION 2: Different Slopes and Intercepts (Non-Parallel Lines)

Variable 1 (Y)	Variable 2 (X)	Line of Best Fit [1]	r^2 Raw	r^2 Corrected for Small Sample
CEM	DPI	$Y = 0.06 - 7.16X_2 + 0.054X + 0.017Z$	0.993	0.992
CEMC	DPIC	$Y = 20.24 - 23.72X_2 + 0.001X + 0.056Z$	0.987	0.986
CEM	TCE	$Y = 0.44 - 7.54X_2 + 0.059X + 0.019Z$	0.994	0.993
CEMC	TCEC	$Y = 18.48 - 21.98X_2 + 0.006X + 0.058Z$	0.989	0.988

[1] Statistical Reference: Johnston, J., *Econometric Methods* (McGraw-Hill, 1963), pp. 221–228.
CEM = Consumer Expenditures for Personal Health Care.
DPI = Disposable Personal Income.
TCE = Total Personal Consumption Expenditures.
Time Period: 1948–1969
X_2 = (0 in each Medicare Year
(1 in each Pre-Medicare Year
$Z = X_2 \cdot X$

all results were highly significant as measured by the r^2 and standard error tests. However, the correlations obtained with assumption 2 (non-parallel lines) yielded the best r^2 values. Note also that the r^2 values so obtained were higher than those using quadratic fits to the data in its entirety as shown in previous tables.

Hence, rather than dealing with a single curvilinear function, the best fit of the data is obtained with two non-parallel linear functions, one during the pre-Medicare era and the other during the post-

[2] Johnston, *Econometric Methods*, pp. 221–228.

Medicare period. The slope of the post-Medicare function is less than that of the pre-Medicare function which indicates that a portion of Consumer Expenditures for Personal Health Care have been transferred from the consumer sector to the governmental sector during the Medicare years.

First Differences

In a further attempt to "de-trend" the data, first differences for Consumer Expenditures for Personal Health Care and Disposable Personal Income were computed. A first difference is defined to be the increase or decrease in the value of a variable from year n to year n+1. The ratios of these first differences were then computed. Ratios were also computed utilizing a one-year time lag for Disposable Personal Income under the assumption that medical expenditures might lag by one year the availability of disposable income.

The results of this analysis are shown in Table 12. It can be seen that these results are not as significant as those obtained using the absolute values of the variables in the previous analyses. However, if extreme values are eliminated from Table 12 and if the one year time lag is used, then even with first differences the ratio only varies from 3.1 percent to 14.5 percent over the twenty-two-year time period.

A correlation analysis of first differences was computed, and the results are shown in Table 13. A significant r^2 was obtained with and without the time lag for the non-deflated data but not for the data expressed in constant dollar terms.

Therefore, even when attempts are made to de-trend the data, the association between what the consumer spends for personal health care and the income available to him remains evident.

Some Preliminary Conclusions

In the article cited previously, Martin Feldstein contends that the consumer is buying an improved product today with his personal health care dollar when compared to that which he bought in 1948.[3] If this is true (and advances in medical technology seem to confirm

[3] Feldstein, "Today's Hospital Costs—What Produced Them?," pp. 6–11.

TABLE 12

Ratios of First Differences
CONSUMER EXPENDITURES FOR PERSONAL HEALTH CARE AND DISPOSABLE PERSONAL INCOME

R1	R2	R3	R4
−64.7%	47.0%	−64.4%	33.3%
1.9	1.8	3.1	2.6
2.9	8.1	3.3	3.5
5.6	2.8	7.0	4.2
5.8	2.6	5.8	3.8
17.0	16.0	13.7	13.1
3.7	2.1	6.2	5.0
6.2	7.4	6.3	5.0
7.3	9.7	8.4	12.3
12.5	26.3	14.2	27.9
7.9	6.0	7.5	4.7
11.0	9.3	7.6	5.4
6.7	3.7	10.6	7.2
7.3	4.6	7.1	5.1
7.6	6.0	14.5	12.4
8.4	6.6	6.2	4.3
5.9	4.3	4.6	−0.3
4.2	−0.3	0.4	−5.7
0.5	−7.5	6.5	2.1
5.0	1.9	8.9	5.0
9.9	8.5	—	—

$R1 = \frac{D1}{D2}$ $R2 = \frac{D3}{D4}$ $R3 = \frac{D1(i+1)}{D2(i)}$ (One year time lag) $R4 = \frac{D3(i+1)}{D4(i)}$ (One year time lag)

D1 = CEM(i+1) − CEM(i)   i = Year
D2 = DPI(i+1) − DPI(i)
D3 = CEMC(i+1) − CEMC(i)   Time Period: 1948–1969
D4 = DPIC(i+1) − DPIC(i)

CEM = Consumer Expenditures for Personal Health Care (Current Dollars)
DPI = Disposable Personal Income (Current Dollars)
CEMC = Consumer Expenditures for Personal Health Care (Constant Dollars)
DPIC = Disposable Personal Income (Constant Dollars)

TABLE 13

Correlation Analysis
FIRST DIFFERENCES: CONSUMER EXPENDITURES FOR PERSONAL HEALTH CARE AND DISPOSABLE PERSONAL INCOME

Variable 1 (Y)	Variable 2 (X)	Line (Curve) of Best Fit	r^2 Raw	r^2 Corrected for Small Sample	Standard Error of Coefficient
D1	D2	Y = 0.31 + 0.048X	0.407	0.348	0.0132
D1(i+1)	D2(i)	Y = 0.48 + 0.44X	0.315	0.247	0.0151
D3	D4	Y = 0.48 + 0.005X	0.004	—	0.0175*
D3(i+1)	D4(i)	Y = 0.67 − 0.009X	0.0143	—	0.0179*

* No significant relationship.
i = Year; Time Period 1948–1969
D1 = CEM(i+1) − CEM(i)—Current Dollars
D2 = DPI(i+1) − DPI(i)—Current Dollars
D3 = CEMC(i+1) − CEMC(i)—Constant Dollars
D4 = DPIC(i+1) − DPIC(i)—Constant Dollars
CEM = Consumer Expenditures for Personal Health Care.
DPI = Disposable Personal Income.

it), then the consumer's major concern with regard to health care should relate to spiraling inflation in the cost of medical services. Stated differently, if health care costs were brought in line with the rest of the economy, that is, if the Medical Price Index were approximately equal to the overall Consumer Price Index, then the consumer sector would be content to spend a fixed percentage of available income for health care.

Many of the articles which deal only with gross increases in health care costs and which do not examine health expenditures in relative income terms are misleading and are not descriptive of actual consumer behavior.

In Chapter 4, the data on consumer spending as presented in this chapter are examined in comparison to consumer spending statistics presented by various interest groups in support of their national health insurance proposals. Some interesting contrasts are noted.

GNP Percentages

The contemporary literature about medical care abounds with statements which discuss the percentage of our Gross National Product (GNP) being spent on health. For example:

> The nation's health and medical care expenditures amounted to $67.2 billion in fiscal year 1970, representing an increase of 12.2% over the health bill for the previous year. A measure of the significance of the amount can be seen in its relationship to the gross national product (GNP). In that year, 7.0% of the market value of all goods and services produced in the United States went for health. Just one year before, the percentage was 6.7.[4]

There are two general problems with most of the published statistics dealing with percentages of GNP spent on health. First, they usually do not include the components of the percentages which would help to account for the increases that have occurred. Second, they tend to aggregate together all types of health-related costs, including research, teaching, public health expenditures, and many others. Yet they give the misleading impression that they are dealing with only personal health care expenditures. This tends to exaggerate the increase in the percentages, since research and public health programs have expanded greatly in recent years.

This chapter analyzes GNP ratios in more detail than does the contemporary literature. First, the ratio of Personal Health Care Expenditures to Gross National Product is examined, including an analysis of the components which make up this ratio. Second, the total personal health care dollar is analyzed by spending agent, i.e., the person or group paying the bill for personal health services. The data developed in this chapter are then compared to some of the popular health statistics from the contemporary medical care literature in Chapter 4.

Personal Health Care Expenditures and Gross National Product

Table 14 presents a series of ratios of personal health care expenditures to Gross National Product in current dollars for the period of this study, 1948 to 1969. It can be seen from the second column of Table 14 that total U.S. Personal Health Care Expenditures as a percentage of GNP have increased from 3.7 percent in 1948 to 5.9 percent in 1969. These percentages are lower than those

[4] Dorothy P. Rice and Barbara S. Cooper, "National Health Expenditures, 1929–70," *Social Security Bulletin* (January, 1971): 3–18.

TABLE 14

RATIOS OF PERSONAL HEALTH CARE EXPENDITURES TO GROSS NATIONAL PRODUCT (Current Dollars)

Year	Total U.S. Personal Health Care Exp.	Total Public Expenditures	Expend. for Medicare	Expenditures for Medicaid and Medical Assistance for the Aged	Other Public Exp.	Total Private Exp.	Consumer Expenditures	Other Private Expenditures
1948	3.7%	0.7%	0.0%	0.0%	0.7%	3.0%	2.9%	0.1%
1949	3.9	0.8	0.0	0.0	0.8	3.1	3.0	0.1
1950	3.8	0.9	0.0	0.0	0.9	3.0	2.9	0.1
1951	3.7	0.9	0.0	0.0	0.9	2.8	2.7	0.1
1952	3.8	1.0	0.0	0.0	1.0	2.8	2.7	0.1
1953	3.8	0.9	0.0	0.0	0.9	2.9	2.8	0.1
1954	4.1	0.9	0.0	0.0	0.9	3.1	3.0	0.1
1955	4.0	0.9	0.0	0.0	0.9	3.0	2.9	0.1
1956	4.1	0.9	0.0	0.0	0.9	3.2	3.1	0.1
1957	4.2	1.0	0.0	0.0	1.0	3.3	3.2	0.1
1958	4.5	1.0	0.0	0.0	1.0	3.5	3.4	0.1
1959	4.6	1.0	0.0	0.0	1.0	3.6	3.4	0.1
1960	4.7	1.0	0.0	0.0	1.0	3.7	3.6	0.1
1961	4.8	1.1	0.0	0.0	1.1	3.8	3.7	0.1
1962	4.8	1.1	0.0	0.0	1.0	3.8	3.7	0.1
1963	4.9	1.1	0.0	0.1	1.0	3.8	3.7	0.1
1964	5.1	1.1	0.0	0.1	1.0	4.0	3.9	0.1
1965	5.1	1.1	0.0	0.1	1.0	4.0	3.9	0.1
1966	5.2	1.3	0.1	0.2	0.9	3.9	3.8	0.1
1967	5.5	1.8	0.6	0.3	0.9	3.7	3.6	0.1
1968	5.7	2.0	0.7	0.4	0.9	3.7	3.6	0.1
1969	5.9	2.1	0.7	0.5	0.9	3.8	3.8	0.1

usually quoted in the contemporary literature. This is because they include only direct personal health services and exclude the other items mentioned above (research, teaching, etc.).

Table 14 also shows the breakdown of GNP ratios by categories. These categories relate to spending agent, i.e., the group or persons paying the bill for health services. The categories are: (1) *Public Expenditures* which is further divided into Medicare, Medicaid, and other public, and (2) *Private Expenditures* which is broken down into two sub-categories, consumer expenditures and other private. Note that Medicaid expenditures include spending under a pre-Medicare Social Security Administration program of Medical Assistance for the Aged.

Table 15 presents the same data in constant dollars with price effect removed. Note that when deflated data are used, the overall ratio of Personal Health Care Expenditures to GNP shows a much smaller increase, from 4.0 percent to 4.7 percent over the twenty-two year period. That is, in current dollar terms approximately two-thirds of the increase in this ratio can be accounted for by escalating prices in the health care field, where increases in health prices have outstripped price increases for the rest of the economy. Figure 3 shows this graphically with the constant dollar curve exhibiting a much flatter slope, indicating a very gradual rate of increase in the ratio. Note that some upswing in the curves occurred during the last four years of the study. This is due to increased expenditures caused

Table 15

RATIOS OF PERSONAL HEALTH CARE EXPENDITURES
TO GROSS NATIONAL PRODUCT
(Constant Dollars)

Year	Total U.S. Personal Health Care Exp.	Total Public Expenditures	Expenditures for Medicare	Expend. for Medicaid and Medical Assistance for the Aged	Other Public Exp.	Total Private Expenditures	Consumer Expenditures	Other Private Expenditures
1948	4.0%	0.8%	0.0%	0.0%	0.8%	3.3%	3.1%	0.1%
1949	4.2	0.8	0.0	0.0	0.8	3.4	3.3	0.1
1950	4.1	0.9	0.0	0.0	0.9	3.2	3.1	0.1
1951	4.2	1.0	0.0	0.0	1.0	3.1	3.0	0.1
1952	4.1	1.0	0.0	0.0	1.0	3.1	3.0	0.1
1953	4.0	1.0	0.0	0.0	1.0	3.0	2.9	0.1
1954	4.1	0.9	0.0	0.0	0.9	3.2	3.1	0.1
1955	4.0	0.9	0.0	0.0	0.9	3.0	2.9	0.1
1956	4.1	0.9	0.0	0.0	0.9	3.2	3.1	0.1
1957	4.3	1.0	0.0	0.0	1.0	3.3	3.2	0.1
1958	4.5	1.0	0.0	0.0	1.0	3.5	3.4	0.1
1959	4.5	1.0	0.0	0.0	1.0	3.5	3.4	0.1
1960	4.5	1.0	0.0	0.0	1.0	3.5	3.4	0.1
1961	4.6	1.0	0.0	0.0	1.0	3.5	3.4	0.1
1962	4.5	1.0	0.0	0.0	0.9	3.5	3.4	0.1
1963	4.5	1.0	0.0	0.1	0.9	3.5	3.4	0.1
1964	4.6	1.0	0.0	0.1	0.9	3.6	3.5	0.1
1965	4.5	1.0	0.0	0.1	0.9	3.6	3.5	0.1
1966	4.5	1.1	0.1	0.2	0.8	3.4	3.3	0.1
1967	4.6	1.5	0.5	0.3	0.8	3.1	3.0	0.1
1968	4.6	1.6	0.5	0.4	0.7	3.0	2.9	0.1
1969	4.7	1.7	0.6	0.4	0.7	3.0	3.0	0.1

by the greater demand for health services resulting from the Medicare and Medicaid programs.

Of greater interest than these overall ratios is the breakdown of the GNP ratios into the categories discussed above. Figure 4 shows this in current dollar terms. It can be readily seen from this chart that most of the increases in the GNP ratio are due to increased public expenditures. These in turn are accounted for by the Medicare and Medicaid programs. Of the total increase of 2.2 percent in the GNP ratio (in current dollars), increased public expenditures accounted for 1.4 percent.

Figure 5 removes price effect and shows the result of expanded governmental programs even more dramatically than Figure 4. If it were not for Medicare and Medicaid, the GNP ratio would have *decreased* in real dollar terms during this period. The overall ratio increased by 0.7 percent, but Medicare and Medicaid together generated a 1.0 percent increase in the ratio; hence, other categories declined.

To briefly summarize this part of the analysis, the oft-quoted increase in GNP ratio appears to be attributable to two major factors. The first and more obvious of these is inflation in health care costs. The second stems from the increased demand (and the services rendered in response to this demand) which has been generated by the Medicare and Medicaid programs. If we remove price effect and measure real productivity, then the ratio has increased only slightly. If we further agree that the purposes of the Medicare and Medicaid programs (providing improved health services for the aged and indigent) are socially desirable, then contemporary society may be overly concerned and even a bit hysterical about the percentage of our Gross National Product being spent on personal health care.

One possible interpretation of these data might be that major policy emphasis should be placed on price containment rather than attempts to control expenditure levels. The data show that expenditure levels have not increased considerably when examined in relative terms. Those increases which are substantial have been for socially desirable programs instituted in recent years.

TOTAL U.S. PERSONAL HEALTH CARE EXPENDITURES
AS A PERCENTAGE OF GROSS NATIONAL PRODUCT

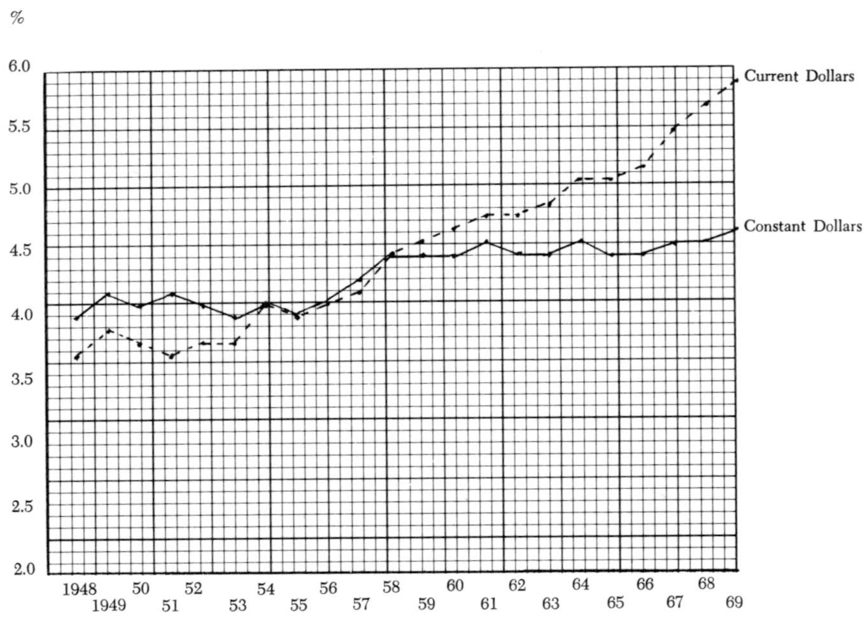

FIGURE 3

U.S. PERSONAL HEALTH CARE EXPENDITURES AS A PERCENTAGE OF GROSS NATIONAL PRODUCT BY FOUR MAJOR SECTORS
(current dollars)

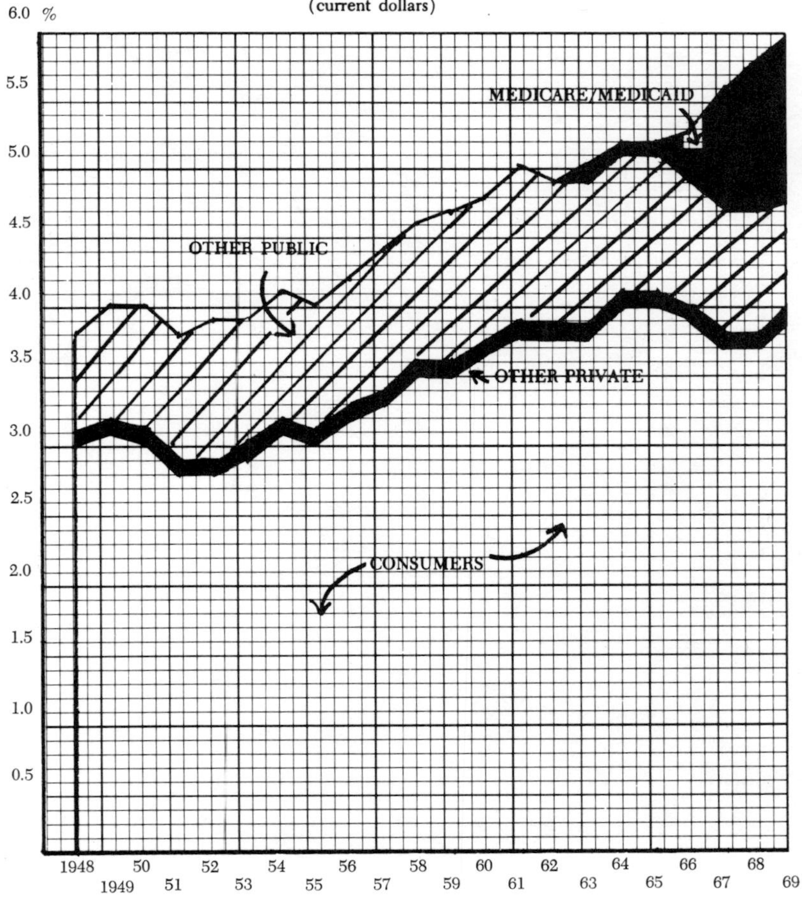

FIGURE 4

U.S. PERSONAL HEALTH CARE EXPENDITURES AS A PERCENTAGE OF GROSS NATIONAL PRODUCT BY FOUR MAJOR SECTORS
(constant dollars)

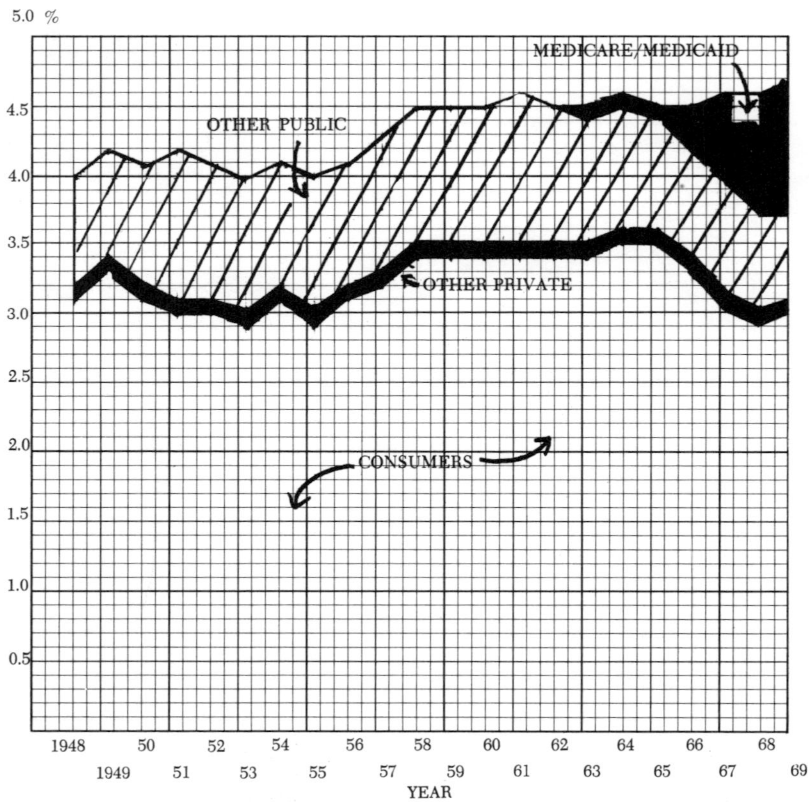

FIGURE 5

The Personal Health Care Dollar

When the U.S. personal health care dollar is examined, a similar picture to that which we have seen in analyzing the GNP ratios emerges. This is particularly true when the dollar is subdivided into spending categories.

Table 16 shows the shift from private to public expenditures for personal health care. Although the private sector still pays the largest part of the bill, the public sector increased from 18.8 percent

TABLE 16

THE PERSONAL HEALTH CARE DOLLAR
1948–1969

Year	Percent Public Expenditures	Percent Private Expenditures	Percent Consumer Expenditures	Percent Medicare and Medicaid
1948	18.8%	81.2%	78.5%	0.0%
1949	19.8	80.2	77.4	0.0
1950	22.4	77.6	74.7	0.0
1951	25.1	74.9	72.1	0.0
1952	25.3	74.7	71.9	0.0
1953	24.0	76.0	73.3	0.0
1954	23.0	77.0	74.3	0.0
1955	22.9	77.1	74.3	0.0
1956	22.8	77.2	74.5	0.0
1957	22.7	77.3	74.7	0.0
1958	22.4	77.6	75.1	0.0
1959	21.8	78.2	75.7	0.0
1960	21.7	78.3	76.0	0.0
1961	22.1	77.9	75.6	0.4
1962	22.0	78.0	75.8	0.9
1963	22.1	77.9	75.7	1.1
1964	21.3	78.7	76.6	1.4
1965	21.0	79.0	77.0	1.7
1966	24.6	75.4	73.5	6.5
1967	33.1	66.9	65.1	16.2
1968	35.5	64.5	62.9	19.4
1969	35.3	64.7	63.2	19.9

in 1948 to 35.3 percent in 1969, while the private sector decreased by a like amount from 81.2 percent to 64.7 percent. The decreased percentage in private expenditures includes the consumer sector which also declined by 15 percent during this period. The decline in the consumer percentage was more than offset by the increases generated by Medicare and Medicaid in the public sector. That is, the government began to pick up expenditures previously paid directly by the consumer.

Table 17 shows the private and public health care dollar when

TABLE 17

	THE PRIVATE PERSONAL HEALTH CARE DOLLAR		THE PUBLIC PERSONAL HEALTH CARE DOLLAR	
Year	Percent Consumer Expenditures	Percent Other Private Expend.	Percent Medicare and Medicaid	Percent Other Public Expend.
1948	96.6%	3.4%	0.0%	100.0%
1949	96.5	3.5	0.0	100.0
1950	96.2	3.8	0.0	100.0
1951	96.2	3.8	0.0	100.0
1952	96.3	3.7	0.0	100.0
1953	96.4	3.6	0.0	100.0
1954	96.4	3.6	0.0	100.0
1955	96.4	3.6	0.0	100.0
1956	96.6	3.4	0.0	100.0
1957	96.7	3.3	0.0	100.0
1958	96.8	3.2	0.0	100.0
1959	96.8	3.2	0.0	100.0
1960	97.1	2.9	0.1	99.9
1961	97.1	2.9	2.0	98.0
1962	97.1	2.9	4.2	95.8
1963	97.2	2.8	5.1	94.9
1964	97.4	2.6	6.4	93.6
1965	97.5	2.5	8.0	92.0
1966	97.5	2.5	26.3	73.7
1967	97.4	2.6	48.8	51.2
1968	97.5	2.5	54.6	45.4
1969	97.7	2.3	56.5	43.5

subdivided further by spending agent. It is interesting to note that the makeup of the private personal health care dollar has not changed during the period of this study. The consumer sector (which includes industrial expenditures for health care for employees) covers 97 percent, with philanthropy picking up the other 3 percent. However, the breakdown of the public dollar has changed. During the first ten to fifteen years of this period (before Medicare and Medicaid), the public dollar was spent by a combination of miscellaneous federal, state, and local programs labeled "Other Public." However, in the latter part of this time period, the Other Public category has declined with the federal dollar for Medicare and Medicaid picking up the difference. It must be emphasized that these data are expressed in relative terms as percentages of total expenditures. This does not mean that state and local programs have declined in overall dollar terms, but only that federal programs are becoming dominant.

This increasing role of the federal government in the financing of health care is a recent phenomenon beginning in 1966 with the advent of Medicare and Medicaid. The percentage of public financing jumped 14 percent in just three years time from 21.0 percent in 1965 to 35.5 percent in 1968. This sudden expansion of federal funding has had two major effects. First, the percentage of health care spending by consumers has declined somewhat since the federal government now pays a large share of the costs of medical care for the aged and poor. However, after an initial period of decline, the consumer portion of the health care dollar seems to be leveling off again at about 65 percent (see Table 16). The second major effect of this increased federal spending seems to be an inflationary one. Figure 4 shows a steep upswing in GNP expenditures devoted to health care from 1966 to 1969, some of which must be attributed to increased demand generated by Medicare and Medicaid. However, it should also be noted that this was a period of rapid inflation for the economy in general. This increased federal funding has also provided some relief to state and local government agencies by absorbing some of the costs previously borne by local welfare sources and municipal hospitals.

COMPARATIVE ANALYSIS 4

Seven major proposals for national health insurance were introduced as bills into Congress during 1971. In addition, three other bills were proposed for coverage of catastrophic illness. These latter plans would relieve the burden of health care costs which exceed a specified dollar limit.

The major political interest groups are lining up support for their positions on national health insurance. These include organized labor, the health insurance industry, consumer groups, the American Medical Association, the American Hospital Association, the American Public Health Association, and several others.

This chapter examines five major proposals for national health insurance in the form in which they were introduced in 1971 and examines the supporting data on health care costs and expenditures which were used in promoting each of the proposals. These health economic data will be compared to those used in the model developed in Chapter 3.

These five proposals are typical of the ones generally thought to have the best chance for passage and the ones which will receive the most serious consideration in Congress. They cover the spectrum from liberal to conservative, and the other bills introduced into Congress are mostly composed of minor modifications to the proposals examined herein. The five proposals are: the National Health Insurance Partnership Act proposed by the Nixon Administration in 1971; the Health Security Program introduced by Senator Kennedy and Representative Griffiths; Medicredit, the American Medical Association proposal; Ameriplan, the American Hospital Association proposal; and Healthcare, the plan developed by the Health Insurance Association of America.

The Nixon Plan

The Nixon Administration proposed a National Health Insurance Partnership, which combined a public and private approach to insurance coverage of the population. Employers would be required to purchase a "standard benefit plan" for their employees, with the employer required to pay 75 percent of the premiums. Some subsidy would be available to the small businessman to assist in paying premiums. The public portion of this bill would be the Family Health Insurance Program which would use federal funds to subsidize health insurance premiums for the poor. Individual cost sharing on the premiums would be required with personal contributions based upon income. Medicaid would be replaced under this plan, but Medicare would be retained.

The benefit package of the National Health Insurance Partnership would include comprehensive hospital and physician's fee coverage. No drugs purchased outside of hospitals and no dental services would be covered, but catastrophic illness protection would be included. The plan would provide extensive co-insurance and deductible provisions designed to help control demand for service which might otherwise result.[1]

[1] Co-insurance is the requirement for the insured to pay a percentage of the cost of the service covered. A deductible is a minimum amount that must first be paid by the insured before coverage of services begins. Co-insurance and deductible provisions are controversial among the various advocates of national

This proposal for national health insurance, a middle-of-the-road approach, would effect some minor changes in the current health delivery system in the United States. The bill would introduce incentives for the establishment of prepaid group practices which the Administration labeled Health Maintenance Organizations. The bill would have minimum effect on hospitals and the private insurance industry with the latter serving as underwriters for the plan. Basically, the 1971 Nixon administration plan would call for continued emphasis on the private health care system rather than the development of an elaborate federalized system of control over the delivery of health care.

Health Security Program

More sweeping changes to the United States health system are proposed in the Health Security Program introduced by Senator Kennedy and Representative Griffiths. Actively supported by organized labor, this bill was originally developed by a committee headed by the late Walter Reuther of the United Auto Workers (The Committee of 100). This committee maintains a full-time staff in Washington, D.C. which is involved in an extensive lobbying effort for the program.

The Health Security Program places emphasis on public control of the health care system. It calls for universal and uniform coverage of the entire population, with no distinction between the poor and other members of society. It would be financed by a combination of general federal tax revenues and a social security type tax on payrolls, with the employer paying the largest share of the payroll tax. Medicare and Medicaid would be eliminated and absorbed into the new system of social insurance.

The bill contains no provision for the use of private insurance carriers. It would be administered through Department of Health, Education and Welfare Regional Offices which would have ex-

health insurance. Some claim that they represent barriers to the receipt of adequate health care. Opponents of this view state that co-insurance and deductible provisions are necessary in order to control demand and indirectly maintain efficient utilization of services.

tensive regulatory powers over the planning and delivery of health services in their region.

The Health Security plan calls for an extensive benefit package including dental services, drugs if obtained through organized out-patient groups, coverage of nursing home and extended care facilities, and home nursing provisions. It includes almost no co-insurance or deductible provisions. Some have questioned the effects of excluding deductibles and co-insurance. Critics of the proposal point to the burgeoning of demand for service under Medicare and the poor cost estimates which resulted from this lack of control over demand.

The Health Security Program would have greater effect on the health delivery system than any of the other proposals, since it would eliminate the private health insurance industry, would place substantial restrictions on the entrepreneurial position of physicians, and would establish an elaborate system of federal governmental regulation of health care. It includes very strong incentives for the group practice of medicine. It calls for the development of national standards within the Department of Health, Education and Welfare which would be used to control providers of health services. Physicians and other providers would not be able to bill patients directly, but rather would have to submit their claims for payment through the federal structure. By eliminating the private health insurance industry in this country, private carriers would be used only as intermediaries for payment purposes. There would be no provision for underwriting by the commercial insurance industry since underwriting would be covered by the federal trust funds to be established under the program.

Medicredit

The American Medical Association has taken an active part in the debate over national health insurance. Realizing the futility of a direct attack such as that waged against Medicare, the AMA decided to fight proposed changes in the practice of medicine by developing its own proposal for national health insurance which it calls Medicredit. Medicredit, as might be expected, calls for continued emphasis on the voluntary system of health services delivery. Tax credits would be granted to individuals for the purchase of private health insurance, with the credits graduated from 99 percent to 10 percent depending on tax liability. The poor would receive insurance certificates redeemable in lieu of cash in order to enable them to purchase private health insurance. The tax credit provisions and the insurance certificates for the poor would be financed by general tax revenues. Medicaid would be absorbed under the AMA proposal. Ironically, Medicare would continue under this plan. It appears that the AMA has changed its opinion about Medicare considerably during the last five years.

The benefits under Medicredit are more limited than those of the Nixon Administration or the Health Security bill. Medicredit would have extensive hospital and physician coverage and some drug coverage on an optional basis. It contains no provisions for dental services or home care. Catastrophic coverage would be optional at additional cost to the insured. The plan calls for extensive deductibles and co-insurance.

Medicredit would have the least effect on the health delivery system of any of the major proposals which have been set forth. It would result in very little interference with the present mode of medical practice. It calls for minimum government control, with the only evaluation of medical care handled on a peer review basis by county medical societies. There would be no change in the role of the private insurance companies other than the requirement to meet some minimum benefit provisions.

Ameriplan

The American Hospital Association entered the debate on health insurance rather late with a hurriedly developed proposal called Ameriplan. Ameriplan calls for a broad restructuring of the health system into approximately 400 Health Care Corporations which would manage the delivery of health care at the local level. All services rendered to individuals in a geographic area would be administered by these corporations, with individual contracts for service developed through insurance mechanisms that would be established. The poor and near poor would be provided free coverage. Others who are financially able would contribute part of the costs of their health insurance premiums. Medicare and Medicaid would be replaced by the new services of the Health Care Corporation.

The plan would be financed by a combination of federal funds and social security tax. It is a controversial proposal and is opposed by the American Medical Association, because it calls for organized corporations to deliver health care. In the opinion of organized medicine, these corporate structures would turn the physician into an "employee" of the corporation with restrictions on his freedom (and possibly his income).

Ameriplan would provide a comprehensive single benefit package including hospital services, physicians' services, extended care facilities, ambulatory care, drugs, and home health services. Dental care would be limited to children, and some catastrophic coverage would be provided.

The effects on the health delivery system would be substantial. The present "cottage industry" of health services delivery would be restructured into an organized system. However, control would reside at the community level through the non-profit Health Care Corporation which would be locally owned and controlled. The private insurance industry could still be used to underwrite the plan. Although not stated directly by its supporters, Ameriplan would provide a major role for local hospitals which would be the logical institutions to provide the organizational and management base required to establish the Health Care Corporation.

Healthcare

The Health Insurance Association of America (representing commercial insurance carriers) introduced into Congress through Rep. Omar Burleson a plan called Healthcare. Healthcare would rely heavily on the private insurance mechanism. Private insurance plans would be financed jointly by employer-employee contributions with tax incentives provided to employers to encourage them to participate in a standard benefit program. State agreements would be formed to cover the poor and near poor on a graduated scale basis depending upon income. This would enable the poor to purchase private insurance policies which would be jointly financed by federal and state funds. Medicaid would be replaced but Medicare would be retained under Healthcare.

The benefit package is extensive. In addition to hospital and physician services, there would be some coverage of dental care, drugs, and home health services. Perhaps because of their underwriting experience, the developers of Healthcare call for extensive use of deductibles and co-insurance in their proposal in order to control demand (and presumably to protect the underwriting of the private insurance companies).

Healthcare would have limited effects on the health delivery system, since it does not propose any major changes to medical practice or the organization of health facilities. Rather, it protects the *status quo* and calls for an expanded role for private insurance companies through tax-subsidized incentives for improved insurance benefits. It does, however, emphasize organized ambulatory care in order to reduce the amount of hospitalization that otherwise would be required. It calls for voluntary planning agencies to control the use of facilities, but also preserves the role of private insurance in the financing of medical care.

Cost Estimates of the Major Proposals

Early in 1971, Secretary Elliot L. Richardson appointed a task force of experts to assist the Department of Health, Education and Welfare in estimating the cost of the proposals for national health insurance that had been introduced into Congress. Most of the staff work for this task force was carried out by economists and statisticians in the Office of Research and Statistics of the Social Security Administration. The task force issued a report in July, 1971, which includes the cost estimates.[2]

Table 18 summarizes the results of the task force cost estimates

[2] U.S. Department of Health, Education and Welfare, *A Study of National Health Insurance Proposals Introduced in the 92nd Congress.* (Supplementary Report to the Congress—includes cost estimates.) Washington, D.C.: Social Security Administration, July, 1971.

TABLE 18

ESTIMATED ANNUAL COSTS OF FOUR PROPOSALS FOR NATIONAL HEALTH INSURANCE
(All Cost Figures in Billions of Dollars)

Plan	Total Cost	Public Cost	Private Cost	Percent Public
National Health Insurance Partnership (Nixon Administration)	$107.2	$44.6	$62.6	41.6%
Health Security Program (Labor/Kennedy Plan)	113.8	97.9	15.9	86.0%
MEDICREDIT (American Medical Association)	109.5	47.6	61.9	43.5%
HEALTHCARE (Private Insurance Industry)	110.2	47.9	62.3	43.5%

NOTE: Estimates are for the Fiscal Year 1974.
SOURCE: U.S. Department of Health, Education and Welfare. *A Study of National Health Insurance Proposals Introduced in the 92nd Congress.* (Supplementary Report to the Congress.) Washington, D.C.: Social Security Administration, July, 1971.

for four of the five plans discussed in this chapter. Since Ameriplan had not yet been introduced into Congress at the time of this study, cost data on this plan were not available.

It is particularly interesting to note the closeness of the estimates for the four plans, which range from $107.2 billion for the Nixon Administration plan to $113.8 for the Health Security Program. These estimates were for fiscal year 1974, assuming a full year of implementation at that time, and, of course, would be much higher if recomputed at this time.

The major difference among the costs of the proposals lies in the breakdown of public and private costs which, of course, reflects the degree of governmental control included in each plan. Note that only the Health Security plan includes substantial governmental control as evidenced by 86 percent of the financing of the plan coming from public funds.

Obviously, the difference in the proportion of government financing leads to major policy differences among the proposals. The Health Security Program would result in substantial government financing and control which could be the first step toward a nationalized medical system. On the other side of the spectrum, the Nixon Administration Program, Medicredit, and Healthcare all call for a majority of the costs (more than 50 percent) to be borne by the private sector. Thus, they would produce public policy which would minimize governmental intervention in the health care system.

Comparison of Health Economic Data

This section will examine data which have been developed in support of the above proposals for national health insurance. The first objective of the analysis is to examine the differences in the kinds of data used to support each proposal. The second objective is to determine the extent to which "rational" analysis supports these proposals, by comparing the economic data presented in support of the plans with that used in the model developed in Chapter 3.

In order to conduct the comparative analysis, an exhaustive page-by-page scan of a large number of documents supporting the major proposals was carried out. The supporting data sources which were examined included the following:

1. The Nixon Administration proposal was analyzed by scanning the President's health message to Congress[3] and a supporting paper developed by the Department of Health, Education and Welfare.[4]
2. A kit of materials was obtained from the Office of the Committee for National Health Insurance in order to analyze data supporting the Health Security Program.[5]

[3] Health Message from the President of the United States. (House Document No. 92–49), U.S. Congress, House of Representatives, 92nd Congress, 1st Session, February 18, 1971 (Washington, D.C.: Government Printing Office, 1971).

[4] U.S. Department of Health, Education and Welfare, *Towards a Comprehensive Health Policy for the 1970's: A White Paper* (Washington, D.C.: Government Printing Office, May, 1971).

[5] Committee for National Health Insurance, *Facts of Life, Health, and Health Insurance* (Washington, D.C.: The Committee, 1969).

3. The American Medical Association central office in Chicago provided a kit of material in support of the Medicredit proposal.[6]
4. Ameriplan is described in a booklet produced by the American Hospital Association which has received wide distribution.[7]
5. The Health Insurance Association provided a kit of material in support of the Healthcare Plan.[8]

In addition to the above material, certain Congressional documents were examined. These included the complete set of hearings of the Kennedy Senate Sub-committee on Health, a ten-volume set of testimony collected by the Sub-committee during hearings held in Washington, D.C. and several other major cities throughout the nation.[9] Although this material is not directly related to the Health Security Program, the biases of the Chairman of the Sub-committee in favor of the labor-sponsored plan which he introduced into Congress are evident in reviewing the testimony. A second document which will play a major role in the debate over national health insurance has been compiled by the House Ways and Means Committee. This Committee started hearings on proposals for national health insurance in the fall of 1971. The Committee on Ways and Means developed a fact book which gives background information on the health care system for the Committee.[10]

The results of the comparative analysis are summarized in the tables which follow. The data are sub-divided into three groups:

[6] American Medical Association, *Medical and Health Care for All: A Description of the Medicredit National Health Insurance Program* (Chicago: The Association, 1971).

[7] American Hospital Association, *AMERIPLAN: A Proposal for the Delivery and Financing of Health Services in the United States* (Chicago: The Association, 1970).

[8] Health Insurance Institute, *Healthcare* (New York: The Institute, 1971) and Health Insurance Institute, *1970 Source Book of Health Insurance Data* (New York: The Institute, 1970).

[9] *Health Care Crisis in America, 1971* (Parts 1 to 10). Hearings before the Subcommittee on Health, Committee on Labor and Public Welfare, U.S. Senate, 92nd Congress (Washington, D.C.: Government Printing Office, 1971).

[10] *Basic Facts on the Health Industry*. U.S. Congress, House of Representatives, 92nd Cong., 1st sess., 28 June 1971 (Washington, D.C.: Government Printing Office, 1971).

first, a comparison of data on consumer expenditures for personal health care; second, an examination of the data on ratios of expenditures to Gross National Product; and third, an examination of data dealing with total U. S. health expenditures.

Table 19 presents comparative data on consumer expenditures

TABLE 19

DATA ELEMENT COVERAGE—CONSUMER EXPENDITURES FOR HEALTH CARE

Data Element	NHI Partnership (Nixon)	Health Security Program (Labor)	MEDI-CREDIT (American Medical Assoc.)	AMERI-PLAN (American Hospital Assoc.)	HEALTH-CARE (Private Insurance Industry)	Kennedy Senate Hearings	House Ways and Means Committee Fact Book
1. Total Consumer Expenditures					X		X
2. Time-trend Data					X		
3. Per capita Expend.							X
4. Deflated Expend.							
5. Expenditures as % of							
—Disposable Income					X		
—Total Consumer Expenditures					X		
—Discretionary Income							
6. Pre/post Medicare							
7. First Differences (yearly increments)							
8. % of population with health insurance	X	X			X	X	X
9. Medical Price Index & Consumer Index	X	X	X		X	X	X

for health care. In comparing the seven data sources with the detailed analysis of consumer spending presented in Chapter 3, it can be seen that the various political advocates have presented sparse data on consumer spending patterns for health care. For example, only the Healthcare proposal of the private insurance industry presents any supporting data which shows the ratio of Consumer Expenditures for Personal Health Care to Disposable Personal Income. None of the proposers presented any data in deflated terms in order to see the effects of removing inflationary factors. None of the advocates examined the differences in consumer spending patterns which occurred before and after Medicare.

Furthermore, none of them considered the percentage of consumer Discretionary Income which is being spent for health services.

Athough the narrative material developed to support the above five proposals contains much rhetoric on the "burden" of health care costs on the consumers, the advocates do a very poor job of documenting these claims with any hard data. As can be seen from Table 19, five of the seven data sources present no data whatsoever on total expenditures by consumers for personal health care.

Table 20 presents similar data on the ratio of health expenditures

TABLE 20

DATA ELEMENT COVERAGE—GROSS NATIONAL PRODUCT RATIOS

Data Element	NHI Partnership (Nixon)	Health Security Program (Labor)	MEDI-CREDIT (American Medical Assoc.)	AMERI-PLAN (American Hospital Association)	HEALTH-CARE (Private Insurance Industry)	Kennedy Senate Hearings	House Ways and Means Committee Fact Book
1. Total Health Expenditures	X	X	X	X		X	X
2. Total Personal Health Care Expenditures							
3. Deflated Expenditures							
4. Breakout by:							
a. Private							
—Consumer							
—Other Private							
b. Public							
—Medicare/ Medicaid							
—Other Public							
5. Pre/post Medicare differences							
6. Other							

to Gross National Product. As can be seen by quickly scanning this table, the data here are even poorer than those of Table 19. In all of the seven data sources, only a single statistic was found; the much-quoted percentage of Gross National Product spent on total health services is cited by six of the seven sources.[11]

The following deficiencies in treatment of this statistic were noted. The data deal only with the percent of GNP spent on total health

[11] Note that this search for data included a complete scan of the ten-volume set of Kennedy Sub-committee hearings which ran to several thousand pages.

services and do not focus in on that portion of total expenditures which go directly for personal health care. That is, no attempt is made to factor out the costs of health manpower, education and training, basic research in the health industry, environmental health programs, etc. Yet these statistics are used in the narrative of these documents as though they deal only with expenditures for personal health care. None of the data sources removed price effect from the ratio in order to examine the effects of inflationary trends. Furthermore, none of the data sources included a breakout by sector, i.e., public, private, consumer, and so forth. None of the sources included differences in the pre- and post-Medicare era which were seen to be significant in the previous chapter.

In summarizing this table, the use of the GNP ratio by the political advocates as a single, isolated statistic covers up the fact that almost all of the increase in the ratio of GNP spent for health can be accounted for by two major factors: inflation in medical care costs and increased demand for health services which have resulted from the Medicare and Medicaid programs.

A somewhat better picture emerges in examining the macro-economic data on total U. S. health expenditures as presented in Table 21. With the notable exception of Ameriplan, fairly complete data on total health expenditures are presented. There are two major deficiencies, however. None of the sources used deflated expenditure data to remove price effect and examine spending patterns in real dollar terms. Only one of the data sources (the House Ways and Means Committee Fact Book) examined pre- and post-Medicare differences in spending patterns. Note also that the data presented in this table focus on total health expenditures (including education, research, public health, etc.) rather than looking at the more immediate question of expenditures for personal health care. The data sources do a fairly good job of presenting the increase in the percentage of expenditures by the public sector, which is noted in six of the seven sources.

In Table 22 nineteen critical data elements are presented. In the judgment of the investigator, a critical data element is one which is needed to present a complete picture of the trends in personal

Table 21

DATA ELEMENT COVERAGE—TOTAL HEALTH EXPENDITURES

Data Element	NHI Partnership (Nixon)	Health Security Program (Labor)	MEDI-CREDIT (American Medical Assoc.)	AMERI-PLAN (American Hospital Assoc.)	HEALTH-CARE (Private Insurance Industry)	Kennedy Senate Hearings	House Ways and Means Committee Fact Book
1. Total Health Expenditures	X	X	X		X	X	X
2. Total Personal Health Care Exp.	X				X		
3. Time-trend Data	X	X	X		X	X	X
4. Per capita expenditures	X	X					X
5. Deflated Expenditures							
6. Pre/post Medicare Differences							X
7. Breakout by type expenditure (Hospital, MD, Drugs, etc.)		X			X		X
8. Percentage Breakdowns							
a. Private	X	X	X		X	X	X
—Consumer					X		X
—Other Private					X		X
b. Public	X	X	X		X	X	X
—Medicare/ Medicaid					X		X
—Other Public					X		X
9. Other							
a. Price Increases in hlth. exp.	X	X	X		X	X	X
b. Third party payments as a % of personal hlth. care exp.	X	X					X
c. Increases in hospital costs	X	X				X	X
d. Increase in federal portion of public hlth. care exp.			X			X	X
e. Spending by age groups							X

health expenditures during the post-World War II period covered by this study. Table 22 summarizes how well each of these nineteen data elements are covered by the seven data sources included in the comparative analysis.

As can be seen from this table, the critical data elements related to consumer expenditures for personal health care are very poorly covered with only one of the elements covered well by the seven data sources. This is item 6, the comparison of the Medical Price Index to the Consumer Price Index. Note that total consumer ex-

TABLE 22

COVERAGE OF CRITICAL DATA ELEMENTS BY SEVEN POLITICAL GROUPS

Data Element	Number of Interest Groups who used this data element	Percent of Interest Groups who used this data element
Consumer Expenditures for Personal Health Care		
1. Total Expenditures	2	29%
2. Post World War II Trend Data	1	14%
3. Removal of Price Effect (Deflated Data)	0	—
4. Expenditures as a percentage of:		
a. Disposable Personal Income	1	14%
b. Total Consumer Expenditures	1	14%
c. Discretionary Income	0	—
5. Pre- and Post-Medicare Differences	0	—
6. Medical Price Index compared to Consumer Price Index	6	86%
Ratios to Gross National Product		
1. Total Health Expenditures	6	86%
2. Personal Health Care Expenditures	0	—
3. Post World War II Trend Data	6	86%
4. Removal of Price Effect (Deflated Data)	0	—
5. Breakout by "Who Pays"	0	—
6. Pre- and Post-Medicare Differences	0	—
Total Health Expenditures		
1. Total Expenditures	6	86%
2. Post World War II Trend Data	6	86%
3. Removal of Price Effect (Deflated Data)	0	—
4. Pre- and Post-Medicare Differences	1	14%
5. Breakouts—Public and Private Spending	6	86%
TOTAL	42	32%

penditures for personal health care are only covered by two of the seven data sources.

The GNP ratios are no better. Only the overall health expenditure items and some trend data related to this statistic are presented. Although total health expenditures receive better treatment by the data sources, the use of aggregated data does not show the important effects of recent trends in health costs and financing on the consumer sector of the population. Overall, only 32 percent or approximately one-third of the critical data elements are covered by the major proposals for revised national health policy.

Table 23 summarizes the data in a different way. This table ranks

TABLE 23

Summary
COVERAGE OF CRITICAL DATA ELEMENTS
RANKED BY POLITICAL GROUP

Political Group	Number of Critical Data Elements Covered	Percent of Critical Data Elements Covered
House Ways and Means Committee	8	42%
HEALTHCARE (Private Insurance Industry)	8	42%
Kennedy Senate Sub-Committee on Health	6	32%
MEDICREDIT (American Medical Association)	6	32%
Health Security Program (Labor/Kennedy)	6	32%
National Health Insurance Partnership (Nixon Administration)	6	32%
AMERIPLAN (American Hospital Association)	2	11%
TOTAL	42	32%

the seven data sources according to how well they covered the nineteen critical data elements. It is interesting to note that the best coverage was presented by the House Ways and Means Committee Fact Book. Since most political observers believe that the results of the House Ways and Means Committee hearings will have major impact on the shape that national health insurance will take, it is encouraging to see good data being developed by this Committee. However, it should also be noted that eleven of the critical data elements (58 percent) were not included in the Committee's fact book. The Healthcare Plan also included similar coverage of eight of nineteen data elements, or 42 percent.

Four of the data sources covered six (32 percent) of the nineteen critical data elements. These were the Kennedy Sub-committee hearings, the Medicredit plan, the Health Security Program, and the National Health Insurance Partnership of the Nixon Administration. Ameriplan had the poorest track record with this data source presenting only two of the nineteen critical data elements. This is somewhat disappointing since Ameriplan calls for a complete restructuring of the health delivery system and yet presents the poorest data to back up the proposal.

To briefly summarize the comparative analysis carried out in this chapter, the adequacy of data on health care expenditures supporting proposals for national health policy is marginal at best. There is inadequate treatment of inflationary effects. There is repeated failure to adequately examine the consumer sector with regard to health care expenditures, and yet this is the sector of the economy which will be directly affected by the proposals and which will provide the necessary political base for the successful plan. There is failure to effectively utilize historical data by examining the before and after effects of Medicare and Medicaid, the first major national health programs which have been implemented in the modern era.

An examination of these data would seem to lend credence to the proposition that "political" factors are probably more important than "rational" analysis in the debate which is developing over a new national health policy. This proposition is examined in detail in Chapter 5.

IMPLICATIONS FOR NATIONAL HEALTH POLICY 5

Utilizing the preceding research results, this chapter extends the investigation to a broader consideration of the policy debate about national health insurance. Much of this discussion is admittedly speculative and based on the author's own views rather than hard empirical evidence. However, the data on how health care costs and finances have been treated in the national health insurance debate suggest that other policy considerations may be treated in similar ways.

The first part is a further review of the five major national health insurance bills discussed earlier, in an attempt to determine the motives behind these proposals. Motives are examined in terms of the hidden agendas of the special interest groups supporting each proposal.

Certain common objectives, shared by all of the national health insurance proposals, are discussed repeatedly in the supporting rhetoric. These objectives tend to be utopian and are difficult to evaluate, since they are abstract and unrelated to specific mechanisms for their implementation. All of the proposals support the concept that health care should be available to all. The idea that "health is a right, not a privilege" is now widely accepted, and the major organizations involved in the national health insurance debate have come to accept this concept and use it as a general objective for promoting their proposals.

There is also universal agreement about the need for improved efficiency in the health delivery system. However, as might be expected, opinions vary widely about the reasons for this lack of efficiency, and no general agreement has been reached about how improved effectiveness can be brought about. Similarly, while there is further agreement about the need to insure high quality health care, there is also considerable disagreement about the mechanisms for insuring that such quality will be present.

Finally, there seems to be general agreement among all of the proposals that the health delivery system should remain pluralistic and acceptable to all segments of society. Most of the proposals emphasize the need for preserving freedom of choice for both patients and the providers of services within the system. None of the national health insurance plans propose a monolithic, government-controlled health system, although some warning flags about this are raised by the more conservative special interest groups involved. Our historical heritage seems to dictate against a nationalized health system, and pluralism will be the hallmark of any proposal that is adopted.

Criteria such as these are prominent in the background material for all the national health insurance proposals reviewed, even from the more conservative groups. For example, the following statement of policy was adopted by the American Medical Association over five years ago:

> It is a basic right of every citizen to have available to him adequate health care; it is a basic right of every citizen to have a free choice of physician and institution. . . . The medical profession, using all means at its disposal, should endeavor to make good medical care available to each person . . . health care

for the poor should not be disassociated from, but rather should be a vital part of, the overall health care system.[1]

The Hidden Agendas

As might be expected, many of the criteria which underlie the various proposals for national health insurance are not stated explicitly. Rather, they represent the "hidden agenda" of the special interest groups involved. An examination of the implicit criteria behind the five major proposals will now be discussed.[2]

Implicit in the thinking behind the 1971 Nixon Administration proposal for National Health Insurance is the need to preserve the private, voluntary aspects of the health care system to the greatest extent possible. Proponents of this proposal would like to avoid large tax increases and simultaneously shun the image of expansionist government programs in our national health policy. The Administration proposal must compete politically with liberal proposals being introduced by members of Congress, particularly the Health Security Program. A further criterion implicit in this proposal is the need to protect certain special interest groups in the health system, particularly the commercial insurance industry. The anti-expansionist view is well summarized in the following quotation:

> Expansionists often take the gradualist or ratchet approach and argue for only a few steps now in the direction of having all health care provided by the government—a system that can truly be called socialized medicine. . . . Realistically, these expansionists recognize that the immediate achievement of their goal would be impossible, both from the legislative likelihoods and from the standpoint of obtaining the cooperation of those who would be needed to provide the necessary services. . . . They hope, however, to "educate" the providers and the public and to establish the conditions so that the movement to social-

[1] Statement of policy adopted by the House of Delegates, American Medical Association, December, 1969.

[2] The criteria are admittedly speculative, based on the author's analysis of each proposal.

ized medicine is inevitable, even though deferred for some years.[3]

A hidden agenda is also behind liberal proposals such as the Health Security Program. One such implicit criterion is the need to minimize out-of-pocket health care costs to workers in organized labor. Also implicit in this plan is consumer rather than provider control of the health care system, with an expanded role for the federal government in more direct control of the system. This need for governmental intervention comes across clearly in a question and answer bulletin distributed by the Committee for National Health Insurance:

> Couldn't these incentives be created without establishing another, massive federal program? No. There are obvious limits to what individual doctors, hospitals, or planning organizations can do when they must rely on voluntary cooperation. . . . Only the federal government can develop a financial lever with sufficient potential to bring change.[4]

Implicit in the Medicredit proposal of the American Medical Association is a strong desire to maintain existing patterns of medical practice in the United States with minimum intervention from the federal government and other outside groups. Also implicit in this plan is continuation of provider rather than consumer control of the health care system. The prerogatives of the professional physician are to be maintained under all circumstances. For example, the AMA wishes to avoid any outside evaluation of the quality of care rendered, and professional peer review is the only acceptable mechanism for maintaining quality within their proposed system. The overall hidden agenda of the AMA plan is to limit national health insurance to a financing system only and to leave the health services delivery system completely as it is today. Such an agenda, of course, is cast in other terms:

[3] Robert J. Myers, "The Spectrum of Governmental Health Care Proposals" (Paper presented to the National Health Insurance Conference, Washington, D.C., July, 1971), pp. 4–5.

[4] Committee for National Health Insurance, *The Physician and Health Security* (Washington, D.C.: The Committee, 1970).

> The American doctor is genuinely concerned that if there is a government health system it will have to compete with other public programs—and in such competition, health care for the American people just might come out second best.[5]

Two major elements are in the hidden agenda of the American Hospital Association's Ameriplan. First, and perhaps most important, is the central role of hospitals in the establishment of health care corporations as called for in the plan. Second is the need to minimize federal control by establishment of non-profit voluntary corporations at the local level. The officers of the AHA clearly see the community hospital as the organizational base for the proposed health care corporations:

> Something like the Health Care Corporation or a Health Maintenance Organization will emerge and while we believe that the Health Care Corporation is the most desirable approach, it is more important to recognize the need for fundamental change than to argue about its details. It is also most important to recognize that the voluntary community hospital will still be the backbone.[6]

The hidden or perhaps not so hidden agenda of the Health Insurance Association of America in its Healthcare plan is to strengthen and preserve the private insurance industry as an integral part of a voluntary health care system. To do so requires minimum government intervention in the delivery and financing of health care. As stated by Mr. J. Henry Smith of the Association in his testimony before the Kennedy Subcommittee hearings on health, March 16, 1971:

> Our program deals realistically with the problems of the existing system, building on its strengths and introducing important changes in a carefully planned manner. . . . Our program preserves the pluralistic approach to both the delivery of care

[5] American Medical Association, *Where Do We Stand?* A Question and Answer Discussion of National Health Issues (Chicago, Illinois: The Association, 1971).

[6] Edwin L. Crosby, "The AHA and Provision of Health Services" (Speech given at the Southeastern Hospital Conference in New Orleans, Louisiana).

and the financing of care, preserves competition and with it the incentive to experiment and innovate.[7]

Renewing the Health Care System

Since the major proposals for national health insurance seem to be based primarily in the hidden agendas of the proposers, it becomes of interest to see how well these plans might fulfill criteria for recognized and needed changes in the health care system.

In order to generalize the discussion and not deal with specific legislative proposals since these change frequently, the analysis in this section examines five kinds of national health insurance proposals which are prototypical of those that have been introduced during the period from 1969 to 1975. The five prototype plans are as follows:

1. *Catastrophic coverage*: Included in this category would be national insurance plans which provide protection against catastrophic illness and which insure that there is no cost beyond a maximum annual family liability. Such plans correspond to private major medical insurance coverage in which all costs, or a substantial percentage of them, are covered once a certain level of expenditure has been reached. These plans are not comprehensive in nature and are relatively inexpensive in terms of the total financing required.

2. *Tax Credit Plans*: These are plans which are designed to provide income tax credit for payment of private health insurance premiums, utilizing a sliding scale based on income. The plans in this category also provide some mechanism for paying private health insurance premiums for the very poor.

3. *Employer-Employee Plans*: These are plans in which private health insurance premiums are shared by employers and employees. Minimum coverage is mandated, and a government subsidy pays insurance premiums for the poor.

4. *Universal Social Security Plans*: These are proposals which involve total coverage of the entire population with costs borne by

[7] *Health Care Crisis in America.* Hearings before the Subcommittee on Health, Committee on Labor and Public Welfare, U.S. Senate, 92nd Congress (Washington, D.C.: Government Printing Office, 1971), part 4, p. 831.

a social insurance tax such as that currently levied for Social Security and Medicare.

5. *Community Corporation Plans*: These are plans which call for restructuring of the local delivery system so that planning and provision of health services are handled by private non-profit corporations. Health insurance premiums paid for by employers and employees will finance the corporation and services rendered.

Figure 6 is a matrix of desirable and needed changes in the health care delivery system. It depicts how well these changes might be achieved by the five prototype national health insurance plans described above. The left column of the matrix indicates the types of changes which are desirable, and the cells of the matrix are coded to indicate whether each of the national health insurance bills

FIGURE 6

EFFECTS OF NATIONAL HEALTH INSURANCE

Legend Ⓥ = substantial effect √ = limited effect O = little or no effect ⊖ = negative effect	CATASTROPHIC COVERAGE (Includes maximum liability plans based on income)	TAX CREDIT PLANS	EMPLOYER/ EMPLOYEE PLANS (with govt. subsidy for poor)	UNIVERSAL SOCIAL-SECUR. PLAN	COMMUNITY CORPORATION PLAN (with contracts for services)
Equalize opportunities for access to medical care	O	√	√	√	√
Help alleviate manpower shortages and maldistribution	O	O	O	√	O
Reduce fragmentation of services & improve coordination among providers	O	O	O	√	Ⓥ
Increase public accountability & consumer role in system	O	O	√	Ⓥ	√
Focus on prevention & health maintenance	O	O	O	√	√
Control rapid increases in costs	O	O	O	⊖	⊖
Improve quality control	O	O	√	√	√
Improve community planning for health services	O	O	O	√	Ⓥ

would have: (1) substantial effect; (2) limited effect; (3) little or no effect: or (4) a negative effect on the desired change. The judgments on effectiveness of each plan are those of the author based upon analysis of the various features of each proposal.

A closer examination of Figure 6 shows that none of the proposals would have substantial, across-the-board effect upon the delivery of health services in the United States. The matrix underlines the fact that national health insurance will provide financing for health care only. It will not bring about major structural changes within the health care delivery system.

Examining the individual proposals, it can be seen that catastrophic coverage would have virtually no effect in bringing about structural changes within the system, and tax credit plans such as Medicredit would also have very little impact upon the way in which health care is delivered in this country. Employer-employee plans based on private insurance would effect only limited change. Universal social security plans and community corporation plans would have the most effect on health care delivery but would not result in *major* changes within the system.

In examining individual structural changes, one can see that most of the proposals would have some limited effect on equalizing opportunities for access to medical care by reducing financial barriers to the receipt of services. The proposals would have very little effect on manpower shortages and maldistribution. With the exception of community corporation plans, the proposals do little to reduce fragmentation of services and improve coordination among the many providers of health care within a community. Some of the proposals would increase public accountability and the role of the consumer in the system, but not to the extent of changing the balance of power among providers and consumers as it is now. Provider control of the system is likely to continue regardless of what form of national health insurance is ultimately enacted. The proposals do not provide much incentive for prevention and health maintenance. None of the proposals would control the rapid increase in costs of health care, and they may tend to bring about more rapid increases in cost. This has been the history of the Medicare program since it was enacted in 1969. Finally, the proposals would have limited effect on improving quality control within the system, and they do not seem to provide incentive for improving community planning.

The analysis is indeed gloomy! It underscores the fact that other programs are needed in addition to national health insurance if we are to develop a health care system that is truly responsive to the needs of all our citizens.

Desirable Criteria for National Health Policy

Since current national health insurance proposals do not seem to provide the panacea, let us turn to a brief consideration of what might be desirable criteria for a national health policy, unconstrained by the limitations of a financing mechanism only. Alice M. Rivlin, former assistant secretary of the Department of Health, Education and Welfare, presents an insightful examination of national health policy in a recent article in the *New York Times* magazine.[8] Rivlin suggests that priorities in our policy mechanisms should be attached to three important changes to be brought about within the health care system. The first of these is to improve health services for the poor. These services are generally recognized to be inadequate and unequal to those of other segments of our society. A second criterion is to prevent the financial effects of catastrophic illness which can attack any citizen regardless of income level. The third needed change is improved efficiency in the health delivery system with control of the costs of health care.

The analysis in this report would indicate that a sound cost control policy would attempt to maintain consumer spending for health services (relative to income) at a constant level. That is, consumers have consistently spent a fixed portion of their income for health services after inflationary effects have been removed, a trend that seems to be well established in the post-World War II period. A system of price controls in which consumer spending is maintained at a constant level relative to income would equalize the ratio of

[8] Rivlin, "Agreed: Here Comes National Health Insurance. Question: What Kind?," 21 July 1974.

total expenditures for personal health care to the Gross National Product. This index would probably level off at about 8 percent.

A sound national policy also should strengthen direct health services for the poor. Such a policy would call for increased direct federal support for neighborhood health centers in rural poverty and inner-city ghetto areas; would strengthen support for public hospitals and long-term care facilities for the poor and aged; would provide direct subsidy for rehabilitative services for those with chronic illnesses; and would provide additional funds for home health services for the poor, aged, and infirm. Note that a comprehensive program of national health insurance could work directly against such a program of improved direct health services for the poor. As more and more of the federal budget is tied up in fixed commitments to a social security trust fund, less of the federal budget becomes available for important categorical programs such as those just mentioned. The recent history of medical care in this country provides ample evidence that, as more and more money is channeled into the social security fund for Medicare, important categorical programs have suffered. In the author's view, reducing financial barriers by providing health insurance will not directly improve the services that are needed for those who are poor, aged, and infirm from chronic illnesses.

The third major aspect of a comprehensive national policy would be the provision of incentives for efficiency. More regulation of providers, both individual physicians and institutions, is needed, but such regulation must be done in a rational way. Systems of prospective reimbursement of providers seem to offer promise for reducing costs, and state regulatory commissions need to be strengthened in their control over the health delivery system. Consumer membership on state regulatory agencies is an essential ingredient.

Finally, improved organization and administration of health services along with strengthened health planning at the community level is essential. In general, we need to move away from the "cottage industry" method of delivery of health services. The system in which physicians and hospitals operate as private entrepreneurs must be replaced by a system in which the buyer of services takes control, perhaps through development of regional health care systems controlled by local citizens.

To summarize, an improved national health policy would include: (1) *no* comprehensive national health insurance, but only catastrophic coverage; (2) direct subsidy to health services programs for the poor, aged, and infirm; and (3) incentives for efficiency through prospective reimbursement, regulation at the state level, and strengthened planning and organization of health services at the community level.

An Important Question

A key question thus develops. Can our policy-making apparatus lead us into "rational" solutions such as those suggested in this chapter, or will we continue to "muddle through" in the special interest advocacy mode of policy-making? A positive answer to this question remains in doubt based upon the way in which the national health insurance debate is progressing. Chapter 6 summarizes the major findings of this study and the implication of these findings for the policy-making process. Included are some suggestions on ways to strengthen and improve our health policy-making apparatus.

SUMMARY AND CONCLUSIONS 6

A recurring theme found both in professional journals and the popular press is that the American health care system is in a state of crisis. The system is beset with many problems. First and most critical of these is the unequal access to health care among different segments of the population. A second problem is fragmentation of health services and lack of coordination among the many providers of health care, both public and private. A third critical element of the health care crisis is the shortage and maldistribution of health manpower throughout the United States, a particularly acute problem in the inner cities and remote rural areas. Finally, much has been written about rapidly rising costs and inefficiency in the allocation and use of scarce resources in the health care field.

As a result of this growing concern about the crisis in health care, health has emerged as a major political issue in the United States. This has been marked by increased involvement from organized consumer groups in the delivery of health services and promotion of the concept that health is a right, not a privilege. Health providers have also reacted to increased criticism in a political fashion. The special interest groups representing organized medicine, hospitals, and the private health insurance industry are all fighting to protect their prerogatives in the health system.

One important result of this growing political debate on the health care system has been the call for a national policy on health. Such a call was the major theme of the 1971 annual meeting of the American Public Health Association. In one of the major addresses at this meeting, the distinguished physician, Dr. Herman Hilleboe, said the following:

> Frankly, there is no national health policy or plan of a comprehensive nature in the U. S. as of October, 1971. . . . A realistic set of long-range health policies, for all to understand and support, would be of immense value to those persons who have to plan and implement health programs at the federal, state and local level. . . . The time is long overdue for a comprehensive health plan for the United States for a ten-twenty year period.[1]

Further evidence of this sudden upsurge of interest in the health care field can be seen in the increasing number of articles in the literature of other disciplines which discuss the health system. For example, the entire January, 1972, issue of the *Annals of the American Academy of Political and Social Science* is devoted to health care.[2] This issue of the *Annals* contains articles by several distinguished authors on the social, political, and economic aspects of the health care system. Included are no fewer than seven papers which deal with costs and expenditures for health services in the United States.

A recurring theme in these papers is that health expenditures have risen rapidly in the period since World War II. Two statistics are widely cited: (1) gross increases in health expenditures, and (2) percent of Gross National Product spent on health. Examples of these kinds of statistics as found in the *Annals* are the following:

[1] Herman E. Hilleboe, "Preventing Future Shock: Health Developments in the 1960's and Imperatives for the 1970's," *American Journal of Public Health* 62 (February, 1972): 142–3.

[2] "The Nation's Health: Some Issues," *Annals of the American Academy of Political and Social Science* 399 (January, 1972).

> Medical care expenditures now absorb in excess of 7 percent of the total national product (GNP), compared to about 5 percent ten years ago.[3]

> The rise in hospital costs is a major reason for the growing public concern about a "health care crisis" in the United States.[4]

> . . . official forecasts indicate that total health expenditures may rise by 1980—less than ten years—from the present level of 7 percent of the Gross National Product to nearly 10 percent . . .[5]

> Expenditures in the health enterprise in the United States are projected to reach between $156 and $189 billion by the end of the current decade. Thus, our society will be spending between 8 percent and 9.8 percent of our Gross National Product for health.[6]

> The United States is currently spending about $75 billions on health care annually. This is approximately 7 percent of our Gross National Product, 32 percent higher than the 5.3 percent in 1960. Health Expenditures increased at an average annual rate of 12.3 percent between 1966 and 1970 compared to a growth rate of 6.3 percent for the economy as a whole.[7]

As a result of these three trends discussed above—growing concern about health services and their cost, emergence of health as a political issue, and calls for a national health policy—several major proposals for a new national health policy have been set forth. All of these proposals call for a program of national health insurance. It is interesting to note that the traditions of voluntarism in the U. S. health system are so strong that even those people calling for the most radical change have limited their proposals to a financing scheme only. No one in the current political debate is calling for an entirely new health delivery system in the United States; the

[3] Sylvester E. Berki and Alan W. Heston, "Introduction," *ibid.*, p. x.

[4] Ronald Andersen and J. Joel May, "Factors Associated with the Increasing Cost of Hospital Care," *ibid.*, p. 63.

[5] Theodore E. Chester, "United States Hospital Costs in International Perspective," *ibid.*, p. 74.

[6] William L. Kissick and Samuel P. Martin, "Issues of the Future in Health," *ibid.*, p. 152.

[7] Anne R. Somers, "The Nation's Health: Issues for the Future," *ibid.*, p. 168.

proposals are limited to those modifications of the system which can be effected by changes to the financing structure.

Methodology of the Study

This study has reviewed one aspect of the call for a new public policy on health by examining two major questions:

1. whether data on health expenditures are being accurately presented by those submitting proposals for a new national health policy; or whether an illusion has been created which overly dramatizes the magnitude of increased spending, and
2. whether the major proposals for national health insurance are based on sound analysis of available data, or whether they are based primarily on the hidden agendas of the special interest groups involved in the debate.

This research has examined one aspect of the policy-making process in the health field. Using background documentation provided by those submitting proposals for national health insurance, the use of macroeconomic data in support of the five major proposals was investigated. The first step in this research was the development of a "rational" model of health expenditures, post-World War II, for comparative purposes. General economic data were collected from U. S. Department of Commerce publications and health economic data were obtained from the Department of Health, Education and Welfare. The data covered a twenty-two-year period from 1948–1969.

The data were summarized and basic ratios were computed. In addition, least-squares curve fitting programs were used to examine the relationship between consumer spending for health care and general consumption expenditures in the economy as a whole. Time-trend analyses were carried out to examine: (1) consumer expenditures for health care in relation to the overall consumer sector of the economy, and (2) total national expenditures for health services relative to the overall economy, particularly as measured by the Gross National Product. The results of these time-trend analyses were then used to produce a simple model of health spending, post-World War II. From the model, nineteen critical data elements were identified which, in the judgment of the investigator, are essential to a complete understanding of health expenditure data for the period under study. The nineteen critical data elements were then compared to data found in the background documentation of the five major proposals for national health insurance in order to see to what extent these proposals were based in sound analyses, and to what extent they were based on the hidden agenda items of the political advocates involved.

Results of the Data Analysis

The first set of data to be examined were consumer expenditures for personal health care. Consumer expenditures when measured in relative terms as a percentage of disposable income, have increased from 3.9 percent in 1948 to 5.5 percent in 1969. However, when price effect is removed, the above ratio increased only slightly from 4.4 percent in 1948 to 5.0 percent in 1965 but declined thereafter (during the Medicare-Medicaid era) to 4.2 percent in 1969. This represents an actual decline in the percentage in real dollar terms of 0.2 percent during the twenty-two-year period.

That is, in real dollar terms, the consumer is spending a smaller proportion of his income after taxes for medical care today than he did twenty-two years ago. The slight decrease in the ratio is due to expanded public expenditures for Medicare which have absorbed some of the funds previously coming from the consumer sector for health care for the aged and poor.

During the period from 1959 to 1969, consumer expenditures for personal health care as a percentage of expenditures from discretionary income (income available for spending after fixed monthly contractual commitments have been met) increased slightly from 12.8 percent to 14.6 percent. However, in real dollar terms, the ratio declined from 12.5 percent to 11.1 percent—due once again to price effect and the effect of increased public expenditures for Medicare.

If we accept the hypothesis that the consumer is buying improved health services today compared to 1948, then the consumer's major concern with regard to health care relates to spiraling inflation in the cost of medical services. Stated differently, if health costs can be brought in line with the rest of the economy (i.e., the Medical Price Index equal to the Consumer Price Index), then the consumer sector would probably be willing to spend a constant percentage of disposable income for health care.

Another statistic which received wide consideration in the literature is the much-cited ratio of total expenditures for health care to Gross National Product. If we consider only expenditures for personal health care in ratio to GNP, we see an increase in this ratio from 3.7 percent in 1948 to 5.9 percent in 1969. However, use of the ratio without qualification is misleading. In real dollar terms with price effect removed, the ratio has increased only slightly from 4.0 percent in 1948 to 4.7 percent in 1969.

Furthermore, when the GNP ratio is examined by its four major components for the same period of time in real dollar terms, the following results are seen. First, the consumer segment declined slightly from 3.1 percent to 3.0 percent of GNP. The "other private" segment remained a constant and negligible 0.1 percent of GNP. The public segment of this ratio excluding Medicare and Medicaid declined slightly from 0.8 percent in 1948 to 0.7 percent of GNP in 1969. The only increase in the ratio (other than that related to price) was caused by the addition of 0.9 percent of GNP for the Medicare and Medicaid programs which went into effect in 1966.

Once again, if health care costs are brought in line with the rest of the economy and if increased demands for service created by Medicare and Medicaid are leveling off, then it is reasonable to expect that the portion of our Gross National Product devoted to health care will also stabilize at some constant percentage.

This analysis points to the importance of examining health economic data in relative terms, i.e., consumer expenditures for health care relative to income and total health care expenditures relative to the resources of the total economy.

Comparing such relative economic statistics to health economic data used by political advocates in supporting proposals for national health insurance shows that these political interest groups have less concern with these types of data analyses. Of nineteen data elements considered critical by the investigator for a complete picture of macroeconomic costs and expenditures in the health care field, an average of only 32 percent or one-third of these data elements were cited in the background material provided by the major proposers of national health policy. In examining seven data sources which were used to support five major proposals for national health insurance, the following results were obtained through comparative analysis:

1. With regard to consumer expenditures for personal health care, a total of eight critical data elements were covered very poorly with only an average of 20 percent of the elements covered by the seven data sources.
2. Data on GNP ratios were not much better. Of a total of six critical data elements in this category, only an average of 29 percent of them were covered by the political interest groups.
3. Data related to an examination of gross total health expenditures were somewhat better. Five critical data elements in this category were covered an average of 63 percent of the time by the seven data sources.

Apparently the hidden agenda items of the political advocates representing their interests and considered prerogatives are more important to the policy-making process than is a broader analysis of the major issues involved.

Conclusions

There are two major conclusions which can be drawn from the research carried out in this study. Simply stated these are:

1. Health expenditures, when converted to real dollar terms, have remained stable relative to the economy as a whole. This constitutes a major departure from current assumptions as discussed in more detail below.
2. The policy-making process in the health field appears to be primarily a process of political advocacy, and much less a process of detailed data analysis.

Let us now consider some of the implications of these two findings.

Finding 1: Magnitude of Expenditure Increases

The finding that health expenditures, when measured as a percentage of total consumption expenditures in constant dollars, have remained stable over time appears to represent a major departure from current assumptions such as those discussed earlier in this chapter. Much misleading information about health expenditures is appearing in both professional journals and the popular press.

As shown by the detailed analyses of this investigation, the small increases in relative consumer spending for health care that have occurred since World War II can be accounted for almost entirely by two factors. One of these is inflation in the health industry and the rapidly rising cost of the delivery of health care. The second is increased demand for service generated by two new federal programs, Medicare and Medicaid, enacted in 1965.

Much attention is being paid to the problem of inflated prices in the health care field. Some of the factors related to rising prices can be explained historically. The biggest portion of the cost of delivery of health care is attributable to personnel costs—salaries, wages, and professional fees. Salaries and wages in the health industry were in a catch-up period during the 1960's. There are indications, however, that the catch-up period is over and that wages in the health industry are now comparable to those in other fields.

Another factor influencing health care costs relates to the technology of medicine. The consumer is buying an improved product today over that which he purchased twenty years ago because of advances in medical knowledge, a fact which tends to be overlooked in examination of health price data over time.

The second variable related to increased health expenditures is the expanded public role in the payment for health services in the United States. The public share of the health care dollar has increased to more than one-third of the total U. S. health expenditures, with all of the increase accounted for by Medicare and Medicaid. These programs have generated some higher spending levels during their initial period of operation because of services which are now more accessible to the aged and the poor. However, this demand for additional health services is leveling off.

It is also interesting to note that the effect of increased public financing of health care has not been only to generate new spending. Most of the increases in public expenditures have simply been a transfer of expenditures previously made by the private sector. For example, the data in this study show that during the pre-Medicare year of 1965, consumer expenditures for personal health care represented 77 percent of total health expenditures. In 1969, four years after the enactment of Medicare and Medicaid, this dropped to 63 percent. Therefore, much of the effect of increased public expenditures resulting from these two programs was simply to transfer funds from one sector of the economy to another. Perhaps the most important lesson to be learned here is that new programs such as these will generate an initial high demand for service which temporarily results in increased spending levels. The planners of such programs would be wise to consider provisions for placing reasonable controls on initial demand generated by new programs.

Finding 2: The Politics of Policy-Making

The second major finding of this study is that the policy-making process in the health field (as in many other areas of public concern) is primarily a process of political advocacy. The results of this research imply that the proposals for national health insurance are based more on the hidden political agendas of the interest groups involved than on detailed analysis of available data, at least so far as economic data are concerned.

Some have argued that the advocacy process in planning and policy-making represents the ideal approach to decision making. One of the major proponents of this point of view is Paul Davidoff who presented the theory of community advocacy planning in 1965.[8] According to Davidoff, competition in the development of proposals for new policies which pluralistic planning would bring about would improve the level of rationality in the policy-making process and

[8] Paul Davidoff, "Advocacy and Pluralism in Planning," *Journal of the American Institute of Planners* 31 (November, 1965): 332.

preparation of the public plan. By acquainting decision-makers with the views of various citizen groups previously imperfectly represented, the advocacy process would expand the criteria upon which plans were set and should be evaluated. The merging of various advocates should then lead to the generation and vigorous defense of several alternatives, and for this reason policy-makers would have a much broader range from which to choose.

An important question thus becomes how well this advocacy theory will work in practice. One empirical study of advocacy planning was carried out by Professor Stephen Skjei in his investigation of the New York City school decentralization debate which took place during the period from 1967 to 1969.[9] The findings of Skjei's study indicate that advocacy systems of planning and policy-making do not necessarily result in improved decisions nor streamline the process of policy making by public bodies.

> Moreover, even if supplemented by a public body which would respond to the informational needs of decision makers, advocacy systems fail to produce a comprehensive picture of the range of alternatives. In many important respects the forums for public debate do not correspond to the institutions of the legal system. The process of public debate only exposes the viewpoints of the participants. It does not necessarily result in the analysis of these viewpoints or in their incorporation into a broad picture of the social costs and benefits of any alternative.[10]

The results of this study show that the data analysis supporting major proposals for national health insurance is inadequate, at least in treatment of health economic data. The poor performance in this one important area leads one to suspect that the same may be true in other kinds of data analysis, i.e., that data analysis properly constructed for examination of the issues in the debate over health policy is generally lacking.

Since there appears to be no great clamor for better data to conduct the debate about policy, the political advocates can concentrate on those aspects of health policy (and related data elements) which

[9] Stephen S. Skjei, "Urban Systems Advocacy," *Journal of the American Institute of Planners* 38 (January, 1972): 11–24.

[10] Skjei, "Urban Systems Advocacy," p. 23.

best serve their interests, rather than conducting a broader examination of all aspects of a proposed new program. Such a conclusion would not concern those supporting the incremental approach to policy-making, who argue that the self-interest advocacy system is in fact the best possible method of policy-making. As Lindblom has stated, every interest will have its watchdog.[11]

This investigator, however, cannot accept the theory of the incrementalists that such a system does in fact protect the interest of every citizen and results in the best possible policy-making. As Lowi has stated:

> When one assumes that "policy making is policy making is decision making" and therefore does not enter into *a priori* analysis of the character of the choices being made, one almost inevitably becomes incrementalist and manipulative. . . . If one does not analyze the character of the choices made, one need not ask any questions about the impact of those choices . . . upon the processes themselves or upon society at large.[12]

This lack of good analytics in the health policy-making process might be explained in two different ways. One explanation might be that policy-makers are deliberately avoiding the analytic approach in order to further their own interest. A second explanation might be that these policy analysis techniques are new and not well-understood, particularly in the health industry which does not have a long tradition of organized planning and management. The answer lies somewhere between these two extremes, with both factors having a role to play in the inadequacy of the analytics of the policy-making process.

The health industry will be the first or second largest industry in the nation by 1980. The use of the newer and more analytical approaches to policy-making in this important social field may be the major challenge facing planners and public policy analysts during the remainder of this decade.

Whether or not the challenge will be accepted remains to be seen.

[11] Lindblom, "The Science of 'Muddling Through,'" p. 85.

[12] Lowi, "Decision Making vs. Policy Making: Toward an Antidote for Technocracy," p. 318.

Historically, there has been reluctance in the Congress and in similar political bodies at the state and local level to engage in any substantive efforts of analysis for social planning purposes. Undoubtedly, this tradition of "nonplanning" will slow the progress that otherwise might occur. However, the literature reviewed for this study shows renewed and expanded interest in policy analysis and contains many calls for better social planning in the United States. This investigator believes that the decade of the 1970's will be the period of slow but steady progress toward the goal of definitive public policy in the health field, increasingly based in careful analysis of the major issues involved.

APPENDIX

Computer Program Listings

1. Print data from Card 1 and compute ratios of Consumer Expenditures for Personal Health Care to general economic measures in the consumer sector.
2. Print data from Card 2.
3. Compute ratios of various health economic measures to Gross National Product.
4. Compute various breakdowns of the medical care dollar.
5. Compute Consumer Expenditures for Personal Health Care as a ratio of Discretionary Income.
6. Compute first differences of Consumer Expenditures for Personal Health Care and Disposable Personal Income.

Punched Card Layouts for Cards 1 & 2

NOTE: All programs written in FORTRAN IV for the IBM 360 Disk Operating System.

```
                    DISK OPERATING SYSTEM/360 FCRTRAN   36CN-FO-451  CL 3-8

C
C PROGRAM TO CCMPUTE BASIC RATICS - MEDICAL ECCNCMIC DATA                AUSTINP1
C PRINT REPORT HEADING                                                   AUSTINP1
      WRITE (3,10)                                                       AUSTINP1
   10 FORMAT (126H1YEAR    GNP        GNPC       DPI        DPIC      TCE AUSTINP1
     1     TCEC       CEM        CEMC       R1         R2         R3     AUSTINP1
     2R4     )                                                           AUSTINP1
C MAIN PROGRAM FCLLCWS                                                   AUSTINP1
   15 READ (1,20) KYR,GNP,DGNP,DPI,DDPI,TCE,DTCE,CEM,DCEM                AUSTINP1
   20 FORMAT (I4,F5.1,F4.1,F6.3,F4.1,F6.3,F4.1,F5.3,F4.1)                AUSTINP1
      IF (KYR-9999) 30,50,50                                             AUSTINP1
   30 GNPC=GNP/DGNP                                                      AUSTINP1
      DPIC=DPI/DDPI                                                      AUSTINP1
      TCEC=TCE/DTCE                                                      AUSTINP1
      CEMC=CEM/DCEM                                                      AUSTINP1
      R1=CEM/DPI                                                         AUSTINP1
      R2=CEMC/DPIC                                                       AUSTINP1
      R3=CEM/TCE                                                         AUSTINP1
      R4=CEMC/TCEC                                                       AUSTINP1
      GNPC=GNPC*100.0
      DPIC=DPIC*100.0
      TCEC=TCEC*100.0
      CEMC=CEMC*100.0
      WRITE (3,40) KYR,GNP,GNPC,DPI,DPIC,TCE,TCEC,CEM,CEMC,R1,R2,R3,R4  AUSTINP1
   40 FCRMAT(1H0,I4,1X,12F10.3)
      GO TO 15                                                           AUSTINP1
   50 STOP                                                               AUSTINP1
      END                                                                AUSTINP1
```

```
                   DISK OPERATING SYSTEM/360 FORTRAN   360N-FO-451   CL 3-8

C                                                                         AUSTINP2
C PROGRAM TO PRINT BASIC DATA - CARD NUMBER 2                             AUSTINP2
C PRINT HEADINGS FOR REPORT                                               AUSTINP2
      WRITE (3,10)                                                        AUSTINP2
   10 FORMAT (117H1YEAR    GNP       TME      PUME      PRME       CEM       EMC   AUSTINP2
     1   EMD      GNPC      TMEC      PUMEC     PRMEC     CEMC      EMCC      EMDC   )  AUSTINP2
C MAIN PROGRAM FOLLOWS                                                    AUSTINP2
      DO 90 I=1,22                                                        AUSTINP2
      READ (1,20) KYR,GNP,DGNP,TME,PUME,PRME,CEM,EMC,EMD,DME              AUSTINP2
   20 FORMAT (I4,F5.1,F4.3,F5.3,F5.3,F5.3,F5.3,F4.3,F4.3,F4.3)            AUSTINP2
      GNPC=GNP/DGNP                                                       AUSTINP2
      TMEC=TME/DME                                                        AUSTINP2
      PUMEC=PUME/DME                                                      AUSTINP2
      PRMEC=PRME/DME                                                      AUSTINP2
      CEMC=CEM/DME                                                        AUSTINP2
      EMCC=EMC/DME                                                        AUSTINP2
      EMDC=EMD/DME                                                        AUSTINP2
      WRITE (3,30)KYR,GNP,TME,PUME,PRME,CEM,EMC,EMD,GNPC,TMEC,PUMEC,PRMEAUSTINP2
     1C,CEMC,EMCC,EMDC                                                    AUSTINP2
   30 FORMAT (1H0,I4,14F8.3)                                              AUSTINP2
   90 GNP=GNP                                                             AUSTINP2
C PREVIOUS STATEMENT DUMMY FOR DO LOOP                                    AUSTINP2
      STOP                                                                AUSTINP2
      END                                                                 AUSTINP2
```

```
                         DISK OPERATING SYSTEM/360 FORTRAN   360N-FO-451  CL 3-8

C                                                                          AUSTINP3
C PROGRAM TO COMPUTE GNP RATIOS                                            AUSTINP3
C PRINT HEADINGS FOR REPORT                                                AUSTINP3
      WRITE (3,10)                                                         AUSTINP3
   10 FORMAT (131H1YEAR   R1     R2     R3     R4     R5     R6     R7     AUSTINP3
     1   R8     R9    R11    R12    R13    R14    R15    R16    R17       RAUSTINP3
     218    R19   )                                                        AUSTINP3
C MAIN PROGRAM FOLLOWS                                                     AUSTINP3
      DO 90 I=1,22                                                         AUSTINP3
      READ (1,20) KYR,GNP,DGNP,TME,PUME,PRME,CEM,EMC,EMD,DME               AUSTINP3
   20 FORMAT (I4,F5.1,F4.3,F5.3,F5.3,F5.3,F5.3,F4.3,F4.3,F4.3)             AUSTINP3
      R1=TME/GNP                                                           AUSTINP3
      R2=PUME/GNP                                                          AUSTINP3
      R3=PRME/GNP                                                          AUSTINP3
      R4=CEM/GNP                                                           AUSTINP3
      R5=(PRME-CEM)/GNP                                                    AUSTINP3
      R6=EMC/GNP                                                           AUSTINP3
      R7=EMD/GNP                                                           AUSTINP3
      R8=(EMC+EMD)/GNP                                                     AUSTINP3
      R9=(PUME-(EMC+EMD))/GNP                                              AUSTINP3
      GNPC=GNP/DGNP                                                        AUSTINP3
      R11=(TME/DME)/GNPC                                                   AUSTINP3
      R12=(PUME/DME)/GNPC                                                  AUSTINP3
      R13=(PRME/DME)/GNPC                                                  AUSTINP3
      R14=(CEM/DME)/GNPC                                                   AUSTINP3
      R15=(PRME/DME-CEM/DME)/GNPC                                          AUSTINP3
      R16=(EMC/DME)/GNPC                                                   AUSTINP3
      R17=(EMD/DME)/GNPC                                                   AUSTINP3
      R18=(EMC/DME+EMD/DME)/GNPC                                           AUSTINP3
      R19=(PUME/DME-(EMC/DME+EMD/DME))/GNPC                                AUSTINP3
      WRITE (3,30)KYR,R1,R2,R3,R4,R5,R6,R7,R8,R9,R11,R12,R13,R14,R15,R16AUSTINP3
     1,R17,R18,R19                                                         AUSTINP3
   30 FORMAT (1HO,I4,18F7.3)                                               AUSTINP3
   90 GNP=GNP                                                              AUSTINP3
C DUMMY STATEMENT FOR DO LOOP                                              AUSTINP3
      STOP                                                                 AUSTINP3
      END                                                                  AUSTINP3
```

```
                  DISK OPERATING SYSTEM/360 FORTRAN   360N-FO-451  CL 3-8

C                                                                   AUSTINP4
C PROGRAM TO CCMPUTE MISC. RATICS - CURRENT DOLLARS                  AUSTINP4
C PRINT HEADING FCR REPCRT                                          AUSTINP4
      WRITE (3,10)                                                  AUSTINP4
   10 FORMAT  (77H1YEAR   R21       R22       R23       R24       R25       RAUSTINP4
     126       R27       R28    )                                   AUSTINP4
C MAIN PROGRAM FCLLCWS                                              AUSTINP4
      DO 90 I=1,22                                                  AUSTINP4
      READ (1,20) KYR,GNP,DGNP,TME,PUME,PRME,CEM,EMC,EMD,DME        AUSTINP4
   20 FCRMAT (I4,F5.1,F4.3,F5.3,F5.3,F5.3,F5.3,F4.3,F4.3,F4.3)      AUSTINP4
      R21=PUME/TME                                                  AUSTINP4
      R22=PRME/TME                                                  AUSTINP4
      R23=CEM/TME                                                   AUSTINP4
      R24=(EMC+EMD)/TME                                             AUSTINP4
      R25=CEM/PRME                                                  AUSTINP4
      R26=EMC/PUME                                                  AUSTINP4
      R27=EMD/PUME                                                  AUSTINP4
      R28=(EMC+EMD)/PUME                                            AUSTINP4
      WRITE (3,30)KYR,R21,R22,R23,R24,R25,R26,R27,R28               AUSTINP4
   30 FCRMAT (1H0,I4,8F9.3)                                         AUSTINP4
   90 GNP=GNP                                                       AUSTINP4
      STCP                                                          AUSTINP4
      END                                                           AUSTINP4
```

```
                    DISK OPERATING SYSTEM/360 FORTRAN   360N-FO-451  CL 3-8

C                                                                        AUSTINP5
C PROGRAM TO COMPUTE RATIOS TO DISCRETIONARY INCOME                      AUSTINP5
C PRINT HEADINGS FOR REPORT                                              AUSTINP5
      WRITE (3,10)                                                       AUSTINP5
   10 FORMAT (65H1YEAR     CEM       CDI         R1        CEMC      CDIC AUSTINP5
     1    R2     )                                                       AUSTINP5
C MAIN PROGRAM FOLLOWS                                                   AUSTINP5
      DO 90 I=1,11                                                       AUSTINP5
      READ (1,20) KYR,DDPI,CEM,DCEM,CDI                                  AUSTINP5
   20 FORMAT (I4,15X,F4.3,10X,F5.3,F4.3,F6.3)                            AUSTINP5
      CEMC=CEM/DCEM                                                      AUSTINP5
      CDIC=CDI/DDPI                                                      AUSTINP5
      R1=CEM/CDI                                                         AUSTINP5
      R2=CEMC/CDIC                                                       AUSTINP5
      WRITE (3,30) KYR,CEM,CDI,R1,CEMC,CDIC,R2                           AUSTINP5
   30 FORMAT (1H0,I4,6F10.3)                                             AUSTINP5
   90 CEM=CEM                                                            AUSTINP5
      STOP                                                               AUSTINP5
      END                                                                AUSTINP5
```

```
                DISK OPERATING SYSTEM/360 FORTRAN   360N-FO-451  CL 3-9
      DIMENSION CEM(22),DCEM(22),DDPI(22),DPI(22)
      DIMENSION D1(21),D2(21),D3(21),D4(21),R1(21),R2(21),R3(21),R4(21)
      WRITE (3,200)
      DO 10 I=1,22
      READ (1,100) DPI(I),DDPI(I),CEM(I),DCEM(I)
      DCEM(I)=CEM(I)/DCEM(I)
      DDPI(I)=DPI(I)/DDPI(I)
   10 WRITE (3,201) CEM(I),DPI(I),DCEM(I),DDPI(I)
      WRITE (3,202)
      DO 20 I=1,21
      D1(I)=CEM(I+1)-CEM(I)
      D2(I)=DPI(I+1)-DPI(I)
      D3(I)=DCEM(I+1)-DCEM(I)
      D4(I)=DDPI(I+1)-DDPI(I)
      R1(I)=D1(I)/D2(I)
      R2(I)=D3(I)/D4(I)
      WRITE (2,210) D1(I),D2(I),D3(I),D4(I)
   20 WRITE (3,201) D1(I),D2(I),D3(I),D4(I)
      WRITE (3,203)
      DO 30 I=1,21
      IF(I-21) 28,29,30
   28 R3(I)=D1(I+1)/D2(I)
      R4(I)=D3(I+1)/D4(I)
      WRITE (2,210) R1(I),R2(I),R3(I),R4(I)
      WRITE (3,201) R1(I),R2(I),R3(I),R4(I)
      GO TO 30
   29 WRITE (2,210) R1(I),R2(I)
      WRITE (3,201) R1(I),R2(I)
   30 CONTINUE
      WRITE (3,204)
      CALL EXIT
  100 FORMAT(13X,F6.3,F4.3,10X,F5.3,F4.3)
  200 FORMAT(1H1,3X,3HCEM,12X,3HDPI,10X,8HCEM/DCEM,7X,8HDPI/DDPI/)
  201 FORMAT(1H0,4(F8.3,7X))
  202 FORMAT(1H1,4X,2HD1,13X,2HD2,13X,2HD3,13X,2HD4/)
  203 FORMAT(1H1,4X,2HR1,13X,2HR2,13X,2HR3,13X,2HR4/)
  204 FORMAT(1H1)
  210 FORMAT(4(F8.3,2X))
      END
```

IBM

INTERNATIONAL BUSINESS MACHINES CORPORATION

MULTIPLE-CARD LAYOUT FORM

Company ______

Application MEDICAL ECONOMIC DATA by C. Austin Date 7/18/71 Job No. ______ Sheet No. ______

KYR	GNP	DGNP	DPI	DDPI	TCE	DTCE	CEM	DME	CDI		CN 1
1–4	5–9	10–13	14–19	20–23	24–29	30–33	34–38	39–42	43–48	49–79	80

CARD NO. 1

KYR	GNP	DGNP	TME	PUME	PRME	CEM	EMC	EMD	DME		CN 2
1–4	5–9	10–13	14–18	19–23	24–28	29–33	34–37	38–41	42–45	46–79	80

CARD NO. 2

NOTE: For definitions of symbols, see Glossary, Table 1

BIBLIOGRAPHY

BOOKS AND MONOGRAPHS

Ackley, Gardner. *Macroeconomic Theory.* New York: Macmillan Co., 1961.

Alchian, Armen A. and Allen, William R. *University Economics.* Belmont, California: Wadsworth Publishing Co., 1967.

American Enterprise Institute for Public Policy Research. *Comprehensive National Medical Care.* Washington, D.C.: The Institute, 1972.

American Hospital Association. *AMERIPLAN: A Proposal for the Delivery and Financing of Health Services in the United States.* Chicago: The Association, 1970.

American Hospital Association. *Analyses of National Health Insurance Proposals.* Chicago: The Association, 1974.

American Medical Association. *Medical and Health Care for All: A Description of the Medicredit National Health Insurance Program.* Chicago: The Association, 1971.

Anderson, Odin W. *The Uneasy Equilibrium: Private and Public Financing of Health Services in the United States, 1875-1965.* New Haven: College and University Press, 1968.

Anderson, Odin W. and May, J. Joel. *The Federal Employees Health Ben-*

efits Program, 1961–1968: A Model for National Health Insurance? Chicago: Center for Health Administration Studies, University of Chicago, 1971.

Battistella, Roger M. and Weil, Thomas P. *Health Care Organization: Bibliography and Guidebook.* Washington, D.C.: Association of University Programs in Hospital Administration, 1971.

Bauer, Raymond A., ed. *Social Indicators.* Cambridge, Mass.: The M.I.T. Press, 1966.

Bennis, Warren G. and Slater, Phillip E. *The Temporary Society.* New York: Harper and Row, 1968.

Booth, S. Lee. *1971 Finance Facts Yearbook.* Washington, D.C.: National Consumer Finance Association, 1971.

Booth, S. Lee. *1970 Finance Facts Yearbook.* Washington, D.C.: National Consumer Finance Association, 1970.

Booth S. Lee. *1969 Finance Facts Yearbook.* Washington, D.C.: National Consumer Finance Association, 1969.

Braybrooke, David and Lindblom, Charles E. *A Strategy of Decision.* New York: The Free Press, 1970.

Brennan, Michael J. *Preface to Econometrics.* Cincinnati, Ohio: Southwestern Publishing Co., 1965.

Bureau of Public Health Economics. *The Economics of Health and Medical Care.* Ann Arbor: University of Michigan, 1964.

Bureau of Public Health Economics. *Medical Care Chart Book.* Ann Arbor: University of Michigan, 1968.

Cohen, Wilbur J. *National Health Insurance: Problems and Prospects.* (The 1970 Michael M. Davis Lecture.) Chicago: Center for Health Administration Studies, University of Chicago, 1970.

Committee for National Health Insurance. *Facts of Life, Health, and Health Insurance.* Washington, D.C.: The Committee, 1969.

Committee on the Costs of Medical Care. *Medical Care for the American People.* Chicago: University of Chicago Press, 1932.

Dernburg, Thomas F. and McDougall, Duncan M. *Macroeconomics.* New York: McGraw-Hill Book Co., 1968.

Falk, Isidores S. *National Policies and Programs for the Financing of Medical Care.* (The 1971 Michael M. Davis Lecture.) Chicago: Center for Health Administration Studies, University of Chicago, 1971.

Feingold, E. *Medicare: Policy and Politics.* San Francisco: Chandler Publishing Co., 1966.

Follmann, J. F. *The Role of Insurance Companies in Financing Hospital Care.* New York: The Health Insurance Council, 1967.

Glaser, William A. *Paying the Doctor.* Baltimore: The Johns Hopkins Press, 1970.

Health Insurance Institute. *Healthcare.* New York: The Institute, 1971.

Health Insurance Institute. *Modern Health Insurance.* New York: The Institute, 1969.

Health Insurance Institute. *1970 Source Book of Health Insurance Data.* New York: The Institute, 1970.

Heilbroner, Robert L. *Understanding Macroeconomics.* Englewood Cliffs, New Jersey: Prentice-Hall, Inc., 1965.

Hirschfield, Daniel S. *The Lost Reform: The Campaign for Compulsory Health Insurance in the United States from 1932 to 1943.* Cambridge, Mass.: Harvard University Press, 1970.

Hoel, Paul G. *Introduction to Mathematical Statistics.* New York: John Wiley & Sons, Inc., 1947.

The Institute of Medicine, National Academy of Sciences. *The Report of the Panel on Implications of a Categorical Catastrophic Approach to National Health Insurance.* Washington, D.C.: National Academy of Sciences, 1973.

Johnston, J. *Econometric Methods.* New York: McGraw-Hill Book Co., 1963.

Kane, Edward J. *Economic Statistics and Econometrics.* New York: Harper & Row, Inc., 1968.

Kennedy, Edward M. *In Critical Condition: The Crisis in America's Health Care.* New York: Simon and Schuster, 1972.

Klarman, Herbert E. *The Economics of Health.* New York: Columbia University Press, 1965.

Kuhn, Alfred. *The Study of Society: A Unified Approach.* Homewood, Illinois: Irwin-Dorsey, 1963.

Lindblom, Charles E. *The Policy Making Process.* Englewood Cliffs, New Jersey: Prentice-Hall, Inc., 1968.

Lyden, Fremont J. and Miller, Ernest G., eds. *Planning, Programming, Budgeting.* Chicago: Markham Publishing Co., 1968.

McNerney, Walter J. *Hospital and Medical Economics.* (Volumes 1 and 2.) Chicago: Hospital Research and Educational Trust, 1962.

McNerney, Walter J. *Improving the Effectiveness of Health Insurance and Prepayment.* Chicago: Blue Cross Association, 1967.

Marmor, Theodore. *The Politics of Medicare.* London: Routledge and Kegan Paul, 1970.

Moynihan, Daniel P. *Maximum Feasible Misunderstanding.* New York: The Free Press, 1970.

National Commission on Community Health Services. *Health Is a Community Affair.* Cambridge, Mass.: Harvard University Press, 1967.

Newhouse, Joseph P. *Policy Options and Impact of National Health Insurance* (R-1528). Santa Monica, California: Rand Corporation, 1974.

Pauly, Mark V. *National Health Insurance: An Analysis.* Washington,

D.C.: American Enterprise Institute for Public Policy Research, 1971.

Phelps, C. E. *The Demand for Health Insurance: A Theoretical and Empirical Investigation* (R-1054). Santa Monica, California: Rand Corporation, 1973.

Price, John R. *et al. National Health Insurance.* Washington, D.C.: American Enterprise Institute for Public Policy Research, 1972.

Remington, Richard D. and Schork, M. Anthony. *Statistics With Applications to the Biological and Health Sciences.* Englewood Cliffs, New Jersey: Prentice-Hall, Inc., 1970.

Richmond, Julius B. *Currents in American Medicine.* Cambridge, Mass.: Harvard University Press, 1969.

Sharkansky, Ira. *Public Administration: Policy Making in Government Agencies.* Chicago: Markham Publishing Co., 1970.

Somers, Anne R. *Health Care in Transition: Directions for the Future.* Chicago: Hospital Research and Educational Trust, 1971.

Somers, Herman N. and Somers, Anne R. *Doctors, Patients, and Health Insurance.* Washington, D.C.: The Brookings Institution, 1961.

Somers, Herman N. and Somers, Anne R. *Medicare and the Hospitals: Issues and Prospects.* Washington, D.C.: The Brookings Institution, 1967.

Spence, Janet T. *et al. Elementary Statistics.* New York: Appleton-Century-Crofts, Inc., 1968.

"The Nation's Health: Some Issues." *Annals of the American Academy of Political and Social Science,* 399 (January, 1972). Entire issue devoted to health care.

Weisbrod, Burton A. *The Economics of Public Health.* Philadelphia: University of Pennsylvania Press, 1961.

Wildavsky, Aaron. *The Politics of the Budgetary Process.* Boston: Little, Brown and Company, 1964.

ARTICLES AND PAPERS

Anderson, Odin W. "The Politics of Universal Health Insurance in the United States." *International Journal of Health Services* 2 (November, 1972): 577-82.

Anderson, Odin W. "Universal and Compulsory Health Insurance: The Last Alternative." *Hospital Administration* 15 (Summer, 1970): 35-53.

Austin, Charles J. "Selected Social Indicators in the Health Field." *American Journal of Public Health* 61 (August, 1971): 1507-13.

Battistella, Roger M. "National Health Insurance: An Examination of

Leading Proposals in the Light of Contemporary Policy Issues." *Inquiry* 8 (June, 1971): 20-36.

Berki, Sylvester E. "Economic Effects of National Health Insurance." *Inquiry* 8 (June, 1971): 37-55.

Berki, Sylvester E. "National Health Insurance: An Idea Whose Time Has Come?" *The Annals of the American Academy of Political and Social Science* 399 (January, 1972): 125-144.

Boulding, Kennneth E. "The Concept of Need for Health Services." *Milbank Memorial Fund Quarterly* XLIV (October, 1966): 202-21

Brierly, Carol. "New Hospital Plan to Reshape Health Care." *Physician's Management* (May, 1971): 51-7.

Burns, Eveline M. "Health Insurance: Not If, or When, But What Kind?" *American Journal of Public Health* 61 (November, 1971): 2164-75.

Catania, James J. "Hospital Costs Are a Bargain." *Hospital Progress* (November, 1968).

Cooper, Barbara S. and McGee, Mary F. "Medical Care Outlays for Three Age Groups: Young, Intermediate, and Aged." *Social Security Bulletin* (May, 1971): 3–14.

Cornely, Paul B. "There is More to Health than Just Paying Bills." (Editorial) *American Journal of Public Health* 64 (September, 1974): 845, 917.

Duesenberry, James S. "Income-Consumption Relations and Their Implications" in *Macroeconomic Readings*, John Lindauer, ed., New York: The Free Press, 1968.

Dunlop, J. T. "Some Facets of the Economics of Health Care Delivery." *Journal of Medical Education* 45 (March, 1970): 133–8.

Ehrenreich, John and Fein, Oliver. "National Health Insurance." *Current* (May, 1971): 24–31.

Feldstein, Martin S. "An Aggregate Planning Model of the Health Care Sector." *Medical Care* (Nov.–Dec., 1967): 369–81.

Feldstein, Martin S. "National Health Insurance: A New Approach." *Public Interest* 23 (Spring 1971): 93–105.

Feldstein, Martin S. "Today's Hospital Costs—What Produced Them?" *Massachusetts Hospital Association Newsletter Supplement* (September, 1971): 6–11.

Feldstein, Paul J. "Applying Economic Concepts to Hospital Care." *Hospital Administration* 13 (Winter, 1968): 68–89.

Garfield, Sidney R. "The Delivery of Medical Care." *Scientific American* 222 (April, 1970): 15–23.

Gorman, Mike. "The Impact of National Health Insurance on Delivery of Health Care." *American Journal of Public Health* 61 (May, 1971): 962–71.

Jaeger, B. Jon. "Government and Hospitals: A Perspective on Health Politics." *Hospital Administration,* no. 1 (1972): 39–51.

Kennedy, Edward M. "National Health Insurance Proposals: Leverage for Change?" *Bulletin of New York Academy of Medicine* 18 (January, 1972): 146–56.

Kindig, David A. and Sidel, Victor W. "Proposed National Health Insurance Programs: Impact on the Consumer." Paper presented to the National Health Insurance Conference at the University of Pennsylvania, Philadelphia (November 12–13, 1970).

Kissick, William L. "Health-Policy Directions for the 1970's." *New England Journal of Medicine* 282 (June 11, 1970): 1343–54.

Klarman, Herbert E. *et al.* "Accounting for the Rise in Selected Medical Care Expenditures, 1929–1969." *American Journal of Public Health* 60 (June, 1970): 1023–39.

Kolodrubetz, Walter W. "Trends in Employee-Benefit Plans in the Sixties." *Social Security Bulletin* (April, 1971): 21–34.

Lampman, Robert J. "Some Comments on the Political and Economic Limits of Health Insurance." *Bulletin of the New York Academy of Medicine* 45 (August, 1969): 738–49.

Levitan, Mark S. *et al.* "A Critique of AMERIPLAN." *Hospital Progress* (May, 1971): 37–60.

Lewis, Charles E. and Keairnes, Harold W. "Controlling Costs of Medical Care by Expanding Insurance Coverage." *New England Journal of Medicine* 282 (June 18, 1970): 1405–12.

Lewis, Irving J. "Government Investment in Health Care." *Scientific American* 224 (April, 1971): 17–25.

Lowi, Theodore. "Decision Making vs. Policy Making: Toward an Antidote for Technocracy." *Public Administration Review* (May–June, 1970).

McNerney, Walter J. "Why Does Medical Care Cost So Much?" *New England Journal of Medicine* 282 (June 25, 1970): 1458–65.

Mosher, Frederick C. "The Public Service in the Temporary Society." *Public Administration Review* (Jan.–Feb., 1971): 47–62.

Mueller, Marjorie S. "Private Health Insurance in 1969: a Review." *Social Security Bulletin* (February, 1971): 3–18.

Myers, Robert J. "The Spectrum of Governmental Health Care Proposals." Paper presented to the National Health Insurance Conference, Washington, D.C. (July 13–14, 1971).

Newhouse, Joseph P. "A Design for a Health Insurance Experiment." *Inquiry* 11 (1974): 5–27.

Newhouse, Joseph P. *et al.* "Policy Options and the Impact of National Health Insurance." *New England Journal of Medicine* 290 (June 13, 1974): 1345–1359.

Pauly, M. V. "An Analysis of Government Health Insurance Plans for Poor Families." *Public Policy* 19 (1971): 489–521.

Prybil, Lawrence. "A Comparison of Six Major Proposals for National Health Insurance." *Hospital Progress* (August, 1971): 48–55.

Rice, Dorothy P. and Cooper, Barbara S. "National Health Expenditures, 1929–70." *Social Security Bulletin* (January, 1971): 3–18.

Robinson, W. S. "Ecological Correlations and the Behavior of Individuals." *American Sociological Review* 15 (1950): 351–7.

Rosett, Richard N. and Huang, L. F. "The Effect of Health Insurance on the Demand for Medical Care." *Journal of Political Economy* 81 (1973): 281–305.

Sgontz, Larry G. "The Economics of Financing Medical Care: A Review of the Literature." *Inquiry* 9 (December, 1972): 5–20.

Somers, Anne R. and Somers, Herman M. "Major Issues in National Health Insurance." *Milbank Memorial Fund Quarterly* 50 (April, 1972): 177–210.

Stevens, Rosemary & Stevens, Robert. "Medicaid: Anatomy of a Dilemma." *Law and Contemporary Problems* 35 (1970): 348–425.

Stone, J. M. "National Compulsory Health Insurance: Time for a Positive Program." *Hospitals* 43 (May 1, 1969): 58–62.

Taylor, Malcolm G. "The Role of the Medical Profession in the Formulation and Execution of Public Policy." *Canadian Journal of Economics and Political Science* 26 (February, 1960).

Tomkins, Richard M. "Evaluating National Health Insurance Legislation: A Summary Review." *Hospital Administration* (Summer 1974): 74–84.

GOVERNMENT DOCUMENTS

Carter, Eugene C. "Health Insurance for the Aged: Amounts Reimbursed by State, 1969." *Health Insurance Statistics.* Washington, D.C. U.S. Department of Health, Education and Welfare, Social Security Administration (October 19, 1971).

Cohen, Wilbur J. *Toward a Social Report.* Washington, D.C.: U.S. Department of Health, Education and Welfare, 1969.

Cooper, Barbara S. "Medical Care Outlays for Aged and Nonaged Persons, 1966–69." *Research and Statistics Note No. 7.* Washington, D.C.: U.S. Department of Health, Education and Welfare, Social Security Administration (June 18, 1970).

Cooper, Barbara S. and McGee, Mary F. "Health Care Outlays for the Young, Intermediate, and Older Age Groups." *Research and Statistics Note No. 17.* Washington, D.C.: U.S. Department of Health, Education and Welfare, Social Security Administration (October 23, 1970).

Cooper, Barbara S. and McGee, Mary F. "National Health Expenditures, Fiscal Years 1929–70 and Calendar Years 1929–69." *Research and Statistics Note No. 25*. Washington, D.C.: U.S. Department of Health, Education and Welfare, Social Security Administration (December 14, 1970).

Council of Economic Advisers. *Economic Report of the President*. Washington, D.C.: Government Printing Office, 1971.

Guralnick, Lillian. "Use of Benefits Under Medicare, 1966 and 1967." *Health Insurance Statistics*. Washington, D.C.: U.S. Department of Health, Education and Welfare, Social Security Administration (April 8, 1971).

Health Care Crisis in America, 1971 (Parts 1 to 10). Hearings before the Subcommittee on Health, Committee on Labor and Public Welfare, U.S. Senate, 92nd Congress, Washington, D.C.: Government Printing Office, 1971.

Health Message from the President of the United States. (House Document No. 92–49), U.S. Congress, House of Representatives, 92nd Congress, 1st Session, February 18, 1971. Washington, D.C.: Government Printing Office, 1971.

Horowitz, Loucele A. "Medical Care Prices Fact Sheet, 1966–1970." *Research and Statistics Note No. 2*. Washington, D.C.: U.S. Department of Health, Education and Welfare, Social Security Administration (March 23, 1971).

Klarman, Herbert E. *et al. Sources of Increases in Selected Medical Care Expenditures, 1929–1969*. Washington, D.C.: U.S. Department of Health, Education and Welfare, Social Security Administration, 1970.

Mueller, Marjorie S. "Enrollment, Coverage and Financial Experience of Blue Cross and Blue Shield Plans, 1969." *Research and Statistics Note No. 4*. Washington, D.C.: U.S. Department of Health, Education and Welfare. Social Security Administration (April 21, 1971).

Reed, Louis S. *Health Insurance Plans Other Than Blue Cross or Blue Shield or Insurance Companies*. Washington, D.C.: U.S. Department of Health, Education and Welfare, Social Security Administration, 1971.

Rice, Dorothy P. and McGee, Mary F. "Projections of National Health Expenditures, 1975 and 1980." *Research and Statistics Note No. 18*. Washington, D.C.: U.S. Department of Health, Education and Welfare, Social Security Administration (October 30, 1970).

Stuart, Bruce C. and Bair, Lee A. *Health Care and Income*. Ann Arbor: State of Michigan, Department of Social Services, 1971.

U.S. Department of Commerce. *Dictionary of Economic and Statistical Terms*. Washington, D.C.: Government Printing Office, 1969.

U.S. Department of Commerce. *The National Income and Product Accounts of the United States,* 1929–1965. Washington, D.C.: Government Printing Office, 1966.

U.S. Department of Commerce. *Survey of Current Business* (National Income Issue). Washington, D.C.: Government Printing Office (July, 1970).

U.S. Department of Health, Education and Welfare. *National Health Insurance Proposals Introduced in the 92nd Congress.* Washington, D.C.: Social Security Administration (May, 1971).

U.S. Department of Health, Education and Welfare. *A Study of National Health Insurance Proposals Introduced in the 92nd Congress* (Supplementary Report to the Congress—includes cost estimates). Washington, D.C.: Social Security Administration (July, 1971).

U.S. Department of Health, Education and Welfare. *Report of the Task Force on Medicaid and Related Programs.* Washington, D.C.: Government Printing Office, 1970.

U.S. Department of Health, Education and Welfare. *Public Attitudes Toward Social Security 1935–1965.* Washington, D.C.: Government Printing Office, 1970.

U.S. Department of Health, Education and Welfare. *Report of the National Conference on Medical Costs.* Washington, D.C.: Government Printing Office, 1968.

U.S. Department of Health, Education and Welfare. *The Size and Shape of the Medical Care Dollar: Chart Book 1969.* Washington, D.C.: Government Printing Office, 1969.

U.S. Department of Health, Education and Welfare. *Towards a Comprehensive Health Policy for the 1970's: A White Paper.* Washingington, D.C.: Government Printing Office, May, 1971.

U.S. Department of Labor. *Handbook of Labor Statistics, 1970.* Washington, D.C.: Government Printing Office, 1970.

U.S. Department of Labor. *Three Standards of Living for an Urban Family of Four Persons.* Washington, D.C.: Government Printing Office, Spring, 1967.

Waldman, Saul. *National Health Insurance: Provisions of Bills Introduced in the 93rd Congress as of October, 1973.* Washington, D.C.: Social Security Administration, Publication No. (SSA) 74–11916, 1973.

Waldman, S. and Peel, E. "National Health Insurance: A Comparison of Five Proposals." *Research and Statistics Note No. 12.* Washington, D.C.: U.S. Department of Health, Education and Welfare, Social Security Administration (July 23, 1970).

Wolfe, Gretchen Y. "Current Medicare Survey Report: Medical Insurance Sample, January–December, 1969." *Health Insurance Statistics.*

Washington, D.C.: U.S. Department of Health, Education and Welfare, Social Security Administration (July 12, 1971).

POPULAR MATERIAL

"Behind the Rising Cost of Health Care." *U.S. News and World Report* 68 (16 March 1970): 63.

"Health Care for Everybody: How Various Plans Would Work." *U.S. News and World Report* 69 (3 May 1971).

"Health Care: Supply, Demand and Politics." *Time* (7 June 1971): 86–93.

"How High Will Hospital Costs Rise?" *Medical World News* 11 (11 December 1970): 33.

Lyons, Richard D. "National Health Insurance Expected Within Three Years." *New York Times* (14 March 1971): 34.

"Mr. Nixon's Health Care Plan." *Newsweek* (1 March 1971).

"Our Ailing Medical System: It's Time to Operate." *Fortune* 81 (January 1970): 78–9.

"Push is on for Added Federal Health Aids." *U.S. News and World Report* (8 February 1971): 35–6.

Ribicoff, Anthony. "Health Care: Rx for Change—The 'Healthiest Nation' Myth." *Saturday Review* 53 (22 August 1970): 18–20.

Rivlin, Alice M. "Agreed: Here Comes National Health Insurance, Question: What Kind?" *New York Times Magazine* (21 July 1974).

Webb, Robert. "Health Plans Flood Senate Hoppers." *Cincinnati Enquirer* (9 May 1971): 12A–13A.

ABOUT THE AUTHOR

Charles J. Austin is Dean of Graduate Studies and Professor of Health Care Administration at Trinity University, San Antonio, Texas. Dr. Austin holds the B.S. degree from Xavier University, Cincinnati, Ohio, the M.S. in Health Administration from the University of Colorado, and the Ph.D. in Interdisciplinary Studies (Social Sciences) from the University of Cincinnati.

Prior to joining the Trinity University administration in 1974, Dr. Austin was on assignment in Washington, D.C. to serve as Study Director for the Commission on Education for Health Administration, an in-depth study of educational programs in health administration and planning funded by the W. K. Kellogg Foundation. From 1969 to 1974 he was a professor in the Graduate Program in Hospital and Health Administration at Xavier University, Cincinnati, Ohio.

Dr. Austin spent seven years, from 1960 to 1967, on various assignments in the U.S. Department of Health, Education and Welfare, including Chief of the Information Systems Division, National Library of Medicine, responsible for the development and operation of MEDLARS, the world's largest operational medical information retrieval system, and as Senior Management Consultant in the Office of the Secretary, HEW. He has also served as Director of Computer Services and assistant professor of Preventive Medicine and Comprehensive Health Care at the University of Colorado Medical Center and as a systems analyst and computer programmer for the Proctor and Gamble Company.

He is a Fellow of the American Public Health Association and a consultant to several federal health programs as well as community health agencies in the San Antonio area. Dr. Austin has published numerous journal articles.